W9-BNS-441

THE QUESTIONING MIND

Faith and values of the new generation

Teija Mikkola – Kati Niemelä – Juha Petterson

Publication 58
Church Research Institute
Tampere 2007

ISBN 978-951-693-281-4
Published by: Church Research Institute, Finland
Printed by: Gummerus Kirjapaino Oy, Jyväskylä, 2007
Cover design: Olli Petterson
Cover photo: Olli Petterson

CONTENTS

1 THE NEW GENERATION SHOWING THE WAY

This book is concerned with religiosity and values among new generations in an urban milieu: in the Helsinki metropolitan area and especially in the Kallio neighbourhood. There are many members of this new generation resident in Kallio. By the new generation we mean those born in the mid 1980s and those age cohorts who were children or young people at that time. At the time of data collection they were approximately thirty years old. The oldest representatives of this generation are those born in 1964, the youngest those born in 1984. They could be called the welfare generation. The oldest in the group, those 30 plus were young in the days of the great breakthrough and spread of consumption. They were the first to live essentially in a consumer culture and take on board the consumer ethos. After them came those of 20 plus, who were young in the age of the 1990s' individualism discussion.[1] The focus of our study is specifically on the generation of Finnish new economic well-being and their values and religious and spiritual worlds. We shall refer to them as young adults.

In recent decades the Finns have witnessed an intense change in economy and information technology: the arrival of the information society, the rise of Technology Finland and the "Nokia Phenomenon". The changes in technology and production economy have been truly remarkable in Finland after the Second World War. The changes, which have occurred in other Western countries, have not been merely structural. The political and ideological changes have been vast.[2] All in all the changes have been so significant and so far-reaching in the West, that we begin to hear of a new age in the history of the world – even of a new era. At first 1989 was taken to be the symbol of the new age.[3] In the

---

1   Hoikkala, Laine & Laine 2005, 16–17.
2   See e.g. Lyon 1995.
3   Beck 1995, 11–12; Lyon 1995, 6. It marked the end of the modern era, which has been delineated as the two hundred years (1789–1989) from the French Revolution to the fall of the Berlin wall.

minds of many this is linked to the demolishing of the Berlin Wall and the unexpected collapse of communist ideology and the communist system.[4] Emphasising structural changes our present Western society has been characterised as postmodern[5], as a service society[6] and now increasingly as an information and knowledge society[7]. The notion of the changed position of knowledge and information in our time is in some way present in many of the interpretations evinced for society today.[8] The changed position of knowledge is also of crucial significance in those interpretations of our age stressing cultural changes alongside structural changes, as in the postmodern discussion.[9]

In recent decades information technology has become part of the Finnish way of life. In the last ten years the majority of Finns have switched over to information and communications technology and the use of the new devices has become a part of everyday routine. In 1996 one household in four had a computer, nowadays two out of three. During the same period there occurred an exponential increase in the number of Internet connections (in 1997 in seven per cent of households, but in 2005 already in 58 per cent). Many Finns use an Internet connection, if not at home, then at least at their workplaces. Computers and the Internet are used more in Finland than in the EU and OECD countries on average. Nowadays almost everyone has a mobile phone (ten years ago there was a mobile phone in four out of ten households).[10]

---

4   Beck 1995, 12–13.
5   Bell 1974.
6   On Finland see e.g. Alestalo 1985, 102–106.
7   The roots of the information society are frequently dated to Japan in the 1960s. The term is thought to have first occurred in Finnish in 1970 in the translation of Peter F. Drucker's work *The Age of Discontinuity.* Anttiroiko, Aro & Karvonen 2000, 23–25.
8   Bell 1974, 112, 487. According to the critis of postmodern society, Daniel Bell among others, a characteristic feature of the new form of society is not only the expansion of service occupations but also the paramountcy of theoretical knowledge in economic and technological growth, likewise the forming of a stratified social structure.
9   E.g. Lyotard 1985, 10–11.
10   http://www.stat.fi/ajk/tiedotteet/v2006/tiedote_017_2006-03-08.html. *Kansalaisesta e-kansalainen. Tilastotutkimusten tuloksia suomalaisten tieto- ja viestintätekniikan käytöstä 1996–2005.*

The Finns living in the front line of information technology adoption are living in a country which for Professor Richard Florida represents a so-called model country of creativity. The capital city, Helsinki, in particular, was an example for Florida of a strongly developing concentration dominated by an ethos of creativity. According to Florida this ethos is also a resource for economic growth. We hope that this study on young Helsinki adults born between 1964 and 1984, their values and religiosity, will help to understand young adults and cultural changes in other countries, too. The book sets out in particular to enhance the understanding of religion and the position of the Church in the lives of young adults. Knowing the beliefs and values of young adults will also help to predict what is to come.

In the background of this research there is a concern for the future. At the beginning of the new millennium increasing attention was paid to the position of young adults in various parts of the Evangelical Lutheran Church of Finland. Most of those resigning from the Church were young adults and in parochial activities the age group was conspicuous by its absence. The share of young adults in the decision-making bodies of the Church was very small. Where are the young adults, why are they not seen in Church activities? Answers to these questions were sought. It was decided to examine young adults in the metropolitan area and especially one neighbourhood in Helsinki, namely Kallio. The choice of this particular research object was underpinned by the assumption that religious and other cultural changes go hand in hand with the growth of the young urban population, that is, the expansion of youth. It was assumed that the changes would manifest themselves in both a questioning of traditional beliefs and Church membership and in the arrival of new forms of spirituality alongside traditional Christianity or instead of it. Kallio was an eminently suitable research area as it is the most urban residential area in Finland and there are a great number of young adults.

The study was an integral part of the three-year project on young adults started up in 2003 by the Parish Union of Helsinki with the following aims:

7

1. To increase and disseminate information and understanding of young adults' lives and life situations.

2. To increase and disseminate information on young adults' values and religiosity

3. To ascertain the numbers of young adults resigning from the Church and joining the Church, the reasons for this and to seek ways of ensuring a positive development in Church membership

4. To learn about the relation between young adults' experiences and expectations and what the parishes are offering and to make development proposals for the parishes activities for young adults.[11]

As a basis for the research, telephone interview data were gathered from 500 young adults (aged 20–39) living in Kallio. The interview questions were connected particularly to religiosity, values and relationship to the Church. In addition to this data, telephone data from 1,000 young adults living in the metropolitan area (Helsinki, Vantaa, Espoo and Kauniainen) collected by the Church Research Institute was used for support.[12] Further to the telephone interviews, personal interviews were conducted with more than a hundred young Kallio adults who had participated in the telephone interviews. Further insight into the values and religiosity of the young adults was sought by comparing the findings with the views of the population as a whole.[13]

The beginning of the research project was characterised by interest in the analysis of the operating environments of the parishes. It emerged that there was very little activity in the Helsinki parishes which was specifically targeted at young adults even though there are many of them living there. Participation in relation to the entire age cohort was also low. Nevertheless it was known in the Helsinki parishes at an early stage in the project that regarding young adults it is not a matter of some superficial

---

11   Halme, Mikkola, Niemelä & Petterson 2006, 6–7.

12   The questionnaire form for the telephone interviews with young adults consisted mostly of the same questions as in Kallio, of somewhat more extensive. Both sets of telephone interviews were done by TNS Gallup. Data collection was in May-June 2004.

13   The comparative data on the entire population was largely that collected by the Church Research Institute for the whole country. These surveys are Gallup Ecclesiastics 2003 (N=1009), Church Monitor 2004 (N=2500) and World Values Survey 2005 (Finland N=1016). Use was also made of opinion polls and statistical data on other subjects.

problem or anything pertaining to activities, but rather something to do with profound religiosity, values and life situation, and even with a widespread change in culture. The findings at the beginning of the project were published in spring 2006 edited by Mikkola, Niemelä and Petterson in a Finnish publication entitled *Urbaani usko – Nuoret aikuiset, usko ja kirkko* (in English: *Urban Faith – Young Adults, Faith and the Church*). This new publication summarises the findings of the projects in English and also goes further. After publication of the book *Urban Faith* we continued to contemplate the matter and endeavoured to delve deep into the world of young adults and get inside their heads in order to understand why the Evangelical Lutheran Church does not seem to appeal to young adults. We considered the development in information technology and the plurality of values, individualisation and the spread of consumer culture and the connection with religion. Our findings are compiled in this book. In it we consider not only what young adults are like, or the nature of their relation to the Church, but also what their world looks like in the eyes of the Church. Our book closes with an epilogue describing how the Church perceives young adults and with what means it has been decided to approach the challenge they pose.

There is a basis for researching urban people and young adults. Big cities have been considered to be the places where innovations come into being and where they proliferate because in big cities the influence of traditions on the human mind is less marked than in rural surroundings. The spatial proximity of people in the cities and the social networks without a place serve to promote the spread of new ideals and models from one to another. Thus the city is the cradle of modernisation, and the new phenomena of modern culture are the outcomes of urban culture. The most susceptible to new influences and those most keen to embrace change are the young age groups on the threshold of adulthood.[14] Among the newest generations the step to adulthood has become longer. The phenomena occurring in this period of less than twenty years have been dubbed the prolonging of youth and the postponement of adulthood. Youth is prolonged over the age of thirty, and being

---

14   See Durkheim 1990, 271–272; Mikkola 2003, 16; Mäenpää 2006, 318.

"really grown up" is only acknowledged after forty.[15] We have extended our examination in this project as far as the age of 39, and 'young adults' is taken to refer to those aged 20–39. Traditionally, 'young adults' has been used to refer to those under 30. This extended group of urban young adults is the one in the front line of societal and cultural changes. They best exemplify the living habits and values which have sought their form in earlier decades and which have now become widespread and matured into their present characteristic form. Young urban adults are the groups which in the sociology literature has frequently been scrutinised as the one to carry out changes in values. Since it is in this economically fairly well placed and well educated group, frequently called the new middle class, that the changes in way of life have progressed farthest, research on them renders understandable what kinds of changes are 'trickling down' to other population groups.

Having gone through the questionnaire data and having personally met young adults, we did not find among them any special ideological system or ideology which was about to spread. Nor did we find any major opposition to ideals or to the Church. What we did find among young adults was not a system of ideals but rather a specific attitude to life: an attitude in which young adults are open to innovations, freely assess various alternatives and arrive at solutions which appear to be the best for oneself and to support one's authentic self. The young adults examined cast doubt on traditional beliefs and values. They were characterised by a critical analysis of their values and identities. They did not blindly follow what they had learned in childhood or beliefs and life models considered eternal truths. They were characterised by a spirit of question and quest. Such *a questioning mind* is unlikely to take support from traditional institutions. Largely self-supporting, it is what *Peter Berger* and co-workers have termed the "homeless" mind.[16]

The critical organisation of one's own identity and the critical analysis of the surrounding world are typical of young adults. On

---

15 See Arnett 2004, 2000.
16 Berger, Berger & Kellner 1977.

the other hand, alongside this questioning spirit there exists in parallel a firm conviction that "anything is possible". They are open to changes and to changing themselves. Young adults live in an affluent society in which, at least materially, many things are possible. The German sociologist *Gerhard Schulze*[17] claims that since we are living in an affluent western society, our lives are governed by choice. The fundamental questions for person making choices in a western consumer society are: What do I really want, and does it please me? Such considerations pave to way to unending self-scrutiny and an emphasis on the experiential in life. However, the everyday pursuit of sensation is not so much geared towards ownership as to being. The precondition for the experiential is the ability to act out some theatrical role or 'destiny'. Since urban life is dominated by variation in social scenes, there is an emphasis in urban life on sensation as varying modes of being.[18] The questioning mind assumes its role in different positions: real or imaginary; own or others; present or possibly future. It is at home in the urban mental atmosphere in which difference is tolerated, likewise different life choices. But constant calling into question may become the captive of continual choice – and constantly long for *something different*. It does not wish to be bogged down in the past, to stagnate, but is ever on the lookout for something new. Being in such a transitory state, and such calling into question, involving the search for one's own identity, concentrating on oneself, imbalance and open opportunities and the interim state are part of the process of becoming adult and are therefore part of the age of young adults. However, in our view, this thinking characteristic of so-called emerging adulthood is prolonged and has made its way elsewhere in the culture. If sometimes the greatest sin has been that of breaking God's commands, now the greatest sin is that of being bogged down in the tried and trusted. Settling down and growing up are not things to be desired in our culture. The content of adulthood has in many ways become unclear, and so has that of religion.

---

17   Schulze 1992.
18   Mäenpää 2006, 320.

FACTS ON FINLAND

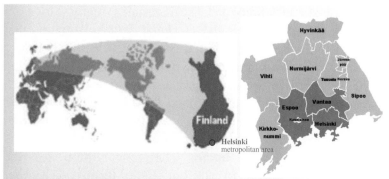

Helsinki
metropolitan area

The Republic of Finland (in Finnish: Suomi, Suomen tasavalta)

Population 5.3 million, 338 000 sq. km
Seventh largest country in Europe and second most northern country
in the world (77% of those 15-74 years used Internet in 2005)
17 inhabitants per sq. km
Independent since December 6, 1917
A member of the European Union since 1995
Currency: euro
Main languages: Finnish, Swedish (5.5%), Russian (0.8%), Estonian (0.3%)
Over 65% of Finland´s land area is covered by forest, 190 000 lakes
GDP: 168 billion euros (2006)
One of the leading countries in Internet use: 71% of Finnish households own a personal computer,
65% have an internet connection and 58% have broadband (77% of those 15-74
years used Internet in 2005)

Capital City: Helsinki 561 000 residents
The Helsinki metropolitan area including the cities of Helsinki, Vantaa, Espoo and
Kauniainen: 990 000 residents
Population density: 1 342.5/km²
The Capital Region (the region of Uusimaa): 1. 2 million residents

Religion:
Main churches: The Evangelical Lutheran Church (82%), The Orthodox Church (1%)
Those baptized as members of Ev. Luth. Church as a percentage of all births in 2006: 84%
Ev. Luth. Church marriages as a percentage of all marriages in 2006: 61%
Ev. Luth. Church funerals as a percentage of all funerals in 2006: about 98%
Attends Church confirmation training in 2006 of all those aged 15: 87%
Attends religious services at least once a month: 15%, attends less than once a year or never:
45% (World Values 2005)
Prays daily: 22%, never prays: 20% (World Values 2005)

11 YOUNG URBAN ADULTS

Young adults

The "new generation" which is the subject of the present study, 20 to 39-year-old residents of the metropolitan area and the Kallio neighbourhood, live in very different and individual life situations. The young subjects, those 20 plus, are living a time of many changes. They are at the point of leaving their childhood homes and the way of life connected to school and the safety net. In front of them is breaking away, going off to study, making a home of their own, starting work and starting a family. It is at this point that the individualisation of values and maturing gets under way. The young people clarify their own values[1] asking themselves who they really are and what they want out of life. The age of 18 years has traditionally been considered a milestone in the development of an individual's values. Up to that point values, that is, the conceptions of desirable objectives and behaviour have been largely an outcome of taking on board the values of parents, relatives, friends and other peers.[2] Another significant age in this formation of values and search for one's own identity has been considered to be 30.[3] This has been considered an age at which adventurous youth ends and adulthood finally arrives.[4] At this

1 Values are concepts or beliefs, pertain to desirable end states or behaviours, transcend specific situations, guide selection or evaluation of behaviour and events, and are ordered by relative importance. Schwatz & Bilsky 1987, 551; Schwartz & Bilsky 1990, 878; Schwartz 1992, 3–4.

2 In social research on changes in values there has been avoidance of young people informants since the individual's system of values has been thought not to take shape before the age of 18. See e.g. Mitchell 1983, 45–46.

3 See e.g. Sheehy 1997, 51, 184–185, Jallinoja 1991, 214–216, Puohiniemi 1993, 19, 24.

4 One way of interpreting youth and young adulthood to observe them through positions achieved on the education, housing, job and pair relationship markets. The starting point of youth might be taken, for example, to be any expression of independence by an adolescent, and the end of youth might then be a recently graduated young adult around thirty who has found him/her self,

point impulsivity is believed to decline and responsibility to increase. At the age of thirty people as if by magic achieve the criteria for being adult: they are economically independent, they make independent decisions and are prepared to accept their own responsibility. They are also expected to have settled by this point into a certain mode of life: a permanent job, a pair relationship and a foot on the housing ladder. The years between 18 and 30 are indeed a time when the individual's values mature, and society permits a life with the advantages of being young.

The years between 18 and 25 have begun to be known in the new developmental psychology as emerging adulthood. The term is intended to make a distinction with extended youth. This is because the years of emerging adulthood differ from youth in that, among other things, one is less under parental supervision and the opportunities for independent experimentation are great. Yet these years are not young adulthood, for "young adulthood" as a concept suggests a state in which early adulthood has already been achieved. However, in the developed Western countries many people of 20 plus, and especially in urban areas, have not assumed positions historically associated with adulthood – especially marriage and parenthood – and many of them think themselves that they have not achieved adulthood. Emerging adulthood has five characteristic traits: It is the age of 1) identity explorations, 2) instability, 3) self-focused age, 4) feeling in-between, 5) possibilities. Although emerging adulthood refers to the life typical between ages 18 and 25, the life characteristic of these years continues right up to age 30.[5]

No stage in life is so introspective as emerging adulthood. The introspection in emerging adulthood is not negative; it is normal, healthy and temporary. This is how an understanding is achieved

---

his/her identity, a permanent home, has started a family and has relatively steady employment. The sociologist Tommy Hoikkala describes the blurring of adulthood when the cultural and social content of adulthood is no longer as clearcut as it once was. Just where youth ends and what middle age is has not been much described in the field of sociology, nor is there consensus on this. Young people seem to slide into adulthood without clear rites of passage. Youth is extended over thirty years of age and one is said to be a "proper" adult only around 40–50. Hoikkala 1989, 134–135; See also Hoikkala 1993; 1994.

5   Arnett 2004; 2000.

of who I am, and what I want from life. It equips people for adult life.[6] But introspection does not necessarily cease once one has lived 25 years. The introspection typical of emerging adulthood also occurs in older age groups, which is in part a consequence of our conditions. We live in a world of many values, with many options, but no ultimate authority to tell us what objective and goal to choose. In the old way it is not a matter of one's life trajectory taking a path on which one tried to make the means fit a given end. Rather it is a matter of which of the attractive objectives primarily presents itself. In new circumstances it is likely that most of the time goes on pondering the selection of objectives rather than on how to achieve an unconsidered goal. The matter of objectives has become extremely important. At the same time it is a constant source of concern, exhausts confidence and creates a paralysing feeling of unending insecurity and so also a state of unceasing restlessness. Bauman claims that we have morality without ethics. According to him ethics is ideally the code which describes the 'universally' right behaviour. Now our belief, among other things in big institutions, in the nature of the Church and the political parties and their ability to provide absolute and binding moral guidelines has vanished.[7]

The Canadian philosopher Charles Taylor calls this subjectification, an increased and ever more complex fixation of attention on the subjects of matters. According to Taylor what is essential for the understanding of present subjectification is to make a distinction between two sides: one of these concerns the mode of action and the other the content of action. The first refers to the defining of objectives or ways of living on the basis of me, which according to Taylor is the inevitable developmental trend in our culture. Nowadays we ourselves must resolve and clarify many things which formerly were defined by external realities and in which we had to be satisfied with the orders issued by authority. Even if the mode of action is determined on the principle of me, the content of action need not be so determined. Objectives need

6   Arnett 2004; 2000.
7   Bauman 1996, 218; Bauman 2002.

not express their own desires and endeavours in opposition to matters external to the self.[8]

Many others have also noted the inevitability of subjectification. According to the sociologist *Ulrich Beck* among others, as the traditional components of identity building decay, individuals are correspondingly compelled to make their own life plans. They are forced to plan, prepare, apply, patch up and repair their life histories.[9] Now human decisions, not old authoritarian structures and traditions determine how to live. It remains for the individual to form his/her own identity. When individualisation is not based on the free decisions of individuals, Beck notes in the manner of Sartre, *"we are condemned to become individual"*. [10] We are condemned to freedom and to make undecided, active solutions.[11] From this it follows that we are also condemned to experience uncertainty in our choices and to seek for new certainties. We are living in the world predicted by Nietzsche in which the old God has died and individuals are increasingly compelled to consider, choose and mould their beliefs, values and norms with their justifications and to bear the uncertainty of their choices.[12] This takes us to the paradox, we have freedom and alternatives to choose, but difficulties in making the choice.[13] *Douglas Coupland*, author of the book *Generation X* about the generation born in the 1960s, brought up by TV, overeducated, undervalued, called this extreme phenomenon getting stuck, a tendency in the face of unlimited choices to opt for none of them. Both young people growing into adulthood and also others encounter difficulty related to making choices.

The content of adulthood is no longer as clear and unclouded. It is not clear where youth ends and middle age begins. Growing up is not tied to chronological age. Formerly growing up and the life order 'normally' associated with it was more clearcut and

---

8   Taylor 1995, 109–110.
9   Beck 1995, 27.
10   Beck 1995, 29.
11   Ortega y Gasset 1963, 58–59.
12   Nietzsche 1995, 360–361.
13   Bauman 2002, 76–77.

unproblematic. In the 1970s a typical 25-year-old had completed education, got married and started a family or was at least expecting the first child and had settled either into working life or motherhood. Nowadays the way to such conceptualised adulthood is much longer. Today's 30-year-olds are yesterday's 20-year-olds.

In order to postpone growing up it has been claimed that the 'credit' granted for being young is now granted for longer. In the West the notion has long dominated that because the young are young, they have more rights than obligations, and now those rights of youth have been extended to ever older age groups. The contemplative state pertaining to that period has also been prolonged. The time for seeking answers to fundamental questions such as the purpose of life, and finding a concrete way of life appropriate to oneself has been extended. A direction in life may be being sought and the responsibility and monotony attendant upon being an adult are avoided in the spirit of "*better old than adult*".

From the perspective of deferred adulthood 30 is not necessarily the magic age at which adventurous youth ends and responsible adulthood begins. Youth is drawn out beyond the age of 30, and "proper adulthood" is only confessed to after 40. When studies are prolonged, when getting a foothold in working life and settling down and especially starting a family are postponed later and later, so also is the inescapable accepting of responsibility for others in addition to oneself. The development of contraception has led us into a world in which cohabiting is part of the life history and numerous premarital sexual relationships are more the rule than the exception. Marriages are made at ever later ages (see Figure 1). The 1970s notion of marrying at 22 actually appears rather odd. At the same time the share of single people has increased. In the same way as marriage is postponed, so also divorce has become more widespread, and the time during which an individual is on the pairing up market has increased.[14] Starting

---

14 In 2004 the average age of women giving birth for the first time was 28 and in Helsinki it was 30 on average (STAKES Statistics 21/2005). In 1970 the corresponding average was 24 years. Paajanen 2002, 10.

families has been postponed so long that for example in Helsinki the average age at delivery of the fist child is over 30. At the same time fewer children are born than before.

Figure 1. Average age of women at delivery of first child and first marriage 1970–2005.

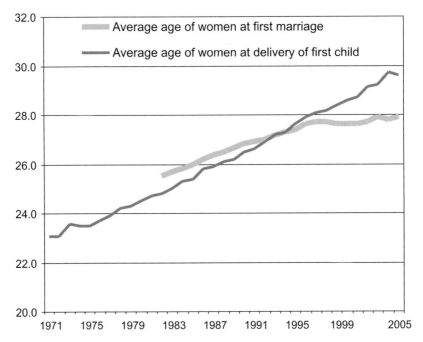

When Finns under 30 were asked why they have not yet had any children the reason given for postponing this was most frequently that they wanted either their own studies or those of the spouse to be completed first. The insecurity of the financial situation and the absence of "being broody" were also common reasons for not having children. In the same survey respondents were asked to estimate why they did not want to have children. The most common reason for choosing not to have children was conjectured to be that it would compromise their independence and emphasising the need to fulfil oneself. The fact that studies take longer to complete and that people want to have their studies finished before the arrival of children was assumed to influence the choice not to have children. Another reason was assumed to be that it is difficult to reconcile the demands of today's working life with having children.[15]

There appear to be many reasons for postponing adulthood, but one explanatory factor has been considered to be that people concentrate more intensely and most productively on work in their younger years, when the prospects for advancement and physical energy are at their zenith. Concurrently time-consuming marriage and the obligation to have children are delayed. In exaggeration, this could be described compared to the lifestyles of earlier generations as the interest-oriented career advancement and postponement of life among young adults today. For many investing in work and career means that work which is considered meaningful makes people willing to do unreasonably long working days. In addition to work, the experiential way of life tempts more and more people to extend the time of their lives when they are without commitment.[16] For young adults the protestant work ethic and the Bohemian ethic are eminently compatible. *"Work hard and play hard"*. Young people putting a great deal into their work see no conflict between systematicity, discipline and having fun. The young adults interviewed constantly had many irons in the fire. Their days were full of various activities as one interviewee graphically put it:

> *Off to study at nine, and I get out at four and after that I'm off like a shot to work at five and I'm there until nine. Then music, photography and films. Music's really my thing.*[17]

Young adults' time is spent on work and having fun, but there is also taking care of one's physical fitness, which in part makes the tough life possible. At the same time marriage is postponed, people are on the pairing off market longer than before. Thus investing in the physical and aesthetic self, frequently considered a manifestation of narcissism, could be practically justified.[18]

---

15   Paajanen 2002, 27, 48.
16   Florida 2005, 59, 279, 305–306; see also Grünstein 2005, 12–13.
17   Kumpulainen & Gothoni 2006, 252.
18   Florida 2005, 59, 279, 305–306; see also Grünstein 2005, 12–13.

From the perspective of the parishes young adults are a challenging group. They typically have no natural contacts to the Church and its activities. The cornerstones of the parishes' activity are community and family. Many young adults are adrift from both of these: they have left their childhood homes, but have not yet attached themselves permanently to a new place of residence. Migration flows to Helsinki and other large cities are strong. Young people also frequently move house within the city. Due to work and studies young adults' communities vary. Nor in the life trajectory of the individual are there natural interfaces to the Church, when marriage and children come later than before.[19]

Urban life

In a cultural sense cities have long been studied on the one hand as causes for alienation, loneliness and social problems and on the other as public spaces for the adaptation of different kinds of people, "melting pots". However, the longstanding suspicion in Finland regarding large cities, especially with the breakthrough in the 1980s of city culture, has turned into an urban enthusiasm. This has been the case among young people in particular. Urbanism is more than mere social space: the proximity of people, the extensive placeless social networks, the public space composed by people unknown to each other and chance encounter. It is also a way of life: different lifestyles and forms which unite. The city is at once the place where different people present themselves and a place in which people learn that the presentation of different selves is also a justified way of being in the world.[20] The presentation of many different selves and tolerating different selves was the essence of urbanism for young people, which broke down their own image of the world.

Urbanism is also life on the markets, and consumption for modern citydwellers has become a way of being in the world. Thus consumption has become an important force forming world view

---

19   Halme & Mikkola & Niemelä & Petterson 2006, 6.
20   Mäenpää 2006, 318–323.

and religiosity. *Mäenpää* talks of a consumer-citydweller. Such a person's life is one long process of choice. It is life in a constant state of choice and being chosen. The consumer-citydweller lives in varying environments and constantly his/her own future prospects. For example, the life of a young adult in Kallio in a broad sense is full of threats related to globalisation (e.g. job loss to countries with lower production costs). However, in a narrower, more personal sense it appears as a series of opportunities stretching to the horizon for the self and pleasant encounters with people, objects, ideologies and thoughts. The individual is constantly confronted by choices and, being reluctant to exclude anything, is disinclined to choose anything. Consuming is not merely buying goods and using them, but a widespread urban habit of encountering the world per se, approaching its phenomena and placing the self in relation to them and of joining society. Urban man is an end in himself and insatiable in his longing and searching. Such is the state to which people have adjusted and which they have learned to be the world order.[21] From this it follows that attaching oneself to a final choice represents a bad life. Then various ties such as that to the spouse, may be too heavy. Indeed, membership of the Church may prove too heavy a tie.

For the consumer, the insatiable person, should she/he feel the Church to be attractive, it is not enough that it offers something for everybody; it must always be offering something *new* for everybody. Therefore, the Church should be like a department store, always with something new on offer.[22]

So where does such a consumer attitude spring from? Pointless consumption is one means of alleviating the monotony of life. The Norwegian philosopher *Lars Fr. H. Svendsen* writes in his work *The Philosophy of Boredom* that we are living in a culture of boredom and that being bored is a typical problem of modern society. According to Svendsen people are not bothered by a certain thing, only nameless, shapeless, formless boredom.[23] For

---

21 Mäenpää 2006, 318–323.
22 Mäenpää 2006, 318–323.
23 Svendson (2005) compares boredom to Freud's description of melancholy. Melancholy and sorrow have a feature in common: both entail a sense of loss.

Svendsen boredom is synonymous with loss of meaning. According to him certain forms of boredom have existed since the beginning of time, for example, boredom connected to concrete daily situations, but boredom connected to loss of meaning is new. Svendsen claims that existential boredom connected to this loss of meaning is fairly exclusively a phenomenon of today's society, and its roots can be traced to the romantic era. Some two hundred years ago, when people began to think of themselves as individual creatures whose purpose was self-fulfilment, the everyday inevitably began to seem like a prison. According to Svendsen boredom is not linked to real needs, but to desire. And that desire is acquire sensations. Sensation is the only "interesting" thing. And it was only towards the end of the age of romanticism at the end of the 1700s that demands appeared to the effect that life should be interesting and that the individual must be able to fulfil themselves. Life must be interesting so as not to be "unbearably boring".[24]

According to Svendsen boredom used to be the bane of the privileged decadent, a problem of the better-off and the intelligentsia; now boredom has spread to wider social strata.[25] Those born into the affluent world after the Second World War have enjoyed all the living space it afforded, something which was previously considered to be the prerogative of the higher minorities.[26] In Svendsen's interpretation boredom is evidence that there is a grave defect in society or culture as a level producing meaning. The derangement of the level producing meanings is manifest in the fact that of the adjective expressing boredom "boring" has become one of the most used linguistic expressions. This has also been used to shed light on several limitations in emotional life and lack of meaning in various situations. It is an indication that there is nothing interesting and how intolerable this

---

The sorrowing individual always has a recognisable object of loss, but the melancholic individual is not so clear as to what s/he has lost. The difference between melancholy and boredom is that boredom does not have the charm of melancholy: melancholy is associated with wisdom, sensitivity and beauty.

24   Svendsen 2005.
25   Svendsen 2005, 9, 13, 17.
26   Cf. Ortega y Gasset 1963, 25.

makes life. Nowadays our interest focuses only on what is interesting, and all that is interesting is that which a moment later will appear indifferent and boring. Indeed, individuality and the everyday are nowadays entwined with one another in a distressing way: the more we emphasise individual life, the more we emphasise the meaning of everyday banalities.[27] Being bored is romantic nostalgia for what we are not, which perhaps does not even exist or which we cannot perhaps even name. Since longing and dissatisfaction are so widespread and comprehensive that we cannot even descry them in front of our very eyes, it is difficult to banish the notion that *something is lacking,* that *we want something more.*[28]

In addition to pointless consumption, leaving or cheating on the spouse is one way of getting something new and filling life's void. Close human relationships and especially love relationships have also become primary environments for self-scrutiny and finding oneself and main forms of self-fulfilment. Love has become a source of identity and a way to find identity.[29] We come to the extreme in the view when human relationships become instrumental and they are deemed tools for advancement. Human relationships may become secondary compared to the self-fulfilment of the individuals involved in them.[30] Then the love relationship may be seen from the perspective of one's own spiritual growth, from the perspective of its potential or occurrence. Earlier people committed to matrimony more out force of habit or necessity and it was to last for life.[31] Now that commitment to matrimony has come to be contemplated from the perspective of one's own inner life a marriage legally binding for

---

27 Svendsen 2005, 9, 13, 17.
28 See Kipnis 2005.
29 Taylor 1995, 63, 71–77.
30 Taylor 1995, 71.
31 Bauman 2002, 142. Cf. Giddens (1991, 88-98; 1995,128; 1999, 61–62) description of the difference of commitment in so-called traditional and so-called pure relationships. Traditional relationships are fixed to social, economic or other external circumstances. Pure relationships live "free-floating" on communication and active choices.

life is not compatible with the likelihood of growth and change. The law of life is changing and not unchanging love.[32]

Public presentation of oneself genuinely and honestly should ethically be the guiding light of life. Thus out of the objective state of affairs caused by the growth of the cities, the melting pot, has come an individual social virtue, tolerance. Appearing honestly and authentically as one's own true self has become the main tenet of a good life, in human relationships and also ethically. This is also required in public life. The city is a place enabling such appearances and the old notion of the city as the "melting pot of nations" has transformed into a positive characteristic of different citydwellers who themselves tolerate difference and of the community in which they have formed.[33] The threats of the city have evolved into promises, and the characteristic features of urban life have become tolerance of difference and unending opportunities. It is the presence of these constant promises and opportunities which is also an indispensable factor making possible the existence of phenomena like that of prolonged youth.[34]

Kallio as the cradle of urban life

It is a characteristic feature of Helsinki that the big age groups of the city are young adults (see Figure 2). The share of young adults is particularly large in the centre, and there especially in Kallio district. Of the population of the Kallio area 30% are aged 20 to 29, and 20% are aged 30–39 (see Figure 3).[35]

---

32 Reich 1972, 367; Mitchell 1983, 155.
33 Mäenpää 2006, 323.
34 Mäenpää 2006, 320–323.
35 Cantell 2006, 12–13, 17.

Figure 2. Population of Helsinki by age group[36]

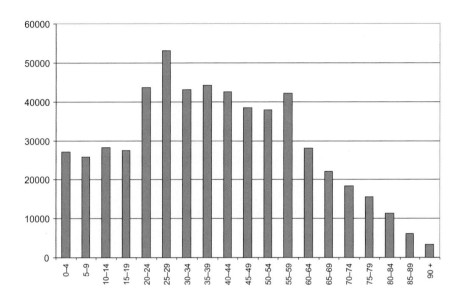

Figure 3. Population of Kallio by age group.[37]

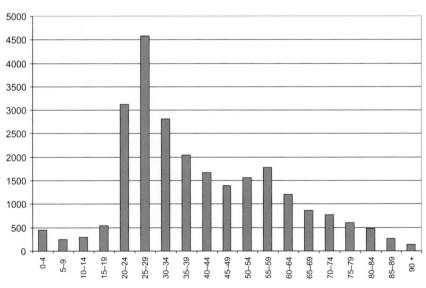

36   Cantell 2006, 13.
37   Cantell 2006, 13.

Kallio, with its population of young adults is a part of town known to many Finns even if they have never been there. It is a neighbourhood which has been made known through writers and other artists. Among others in the film *Calamari Union* by the film director *Aki Kaurismäki*, the cameras are turned on Kallio, once the home of the working classes. In addition to left wing politics and working class milieu an easy, Bohemian pace is a trait which many locals associate with Kallio. Kallio, as stated in the country's main quality daily, is the most romanticised urban district in Finland, which fascinates writers and other artists, rural Finns moving to Helsinki and all manner of potential easy riders.[38]

The dubious reputation of Kallio is enshrined in a trinity of sex, drugs and bars. In Kallio they abound. On the other hand, it is a positive characteristic of Kallio that all sorts of lives are lived there and that this is tolerated. Difference and toleration of difference, as is noted in the Kallio homepages, is a positive urban feature.[39] Many kinds of artists and young adults enjoy living in the relaxed Kallio atmosphere. This former working class neighbourhood now populated by the new generation has over the years undergone an expansion of the middle-class, rejuvenation and has become politically greener.

For young adults Kallio is a pleasant part of town as it is close to the centre, there are plenty of friends and neighbours of the same age and the housing prices are not as high as elsewhere in the city area. The housing prices are due in part to the small size of the apartments. Almost 90% of the flats in Kallio are studios or two-roomed flats with no kitchen. The average living area per flat is 30 square metres per person. Living in Kallio is and always has been cramped. By both Finnish and European standards people live exceptionally close together. If the industrial areas are subtracted, the population density of Kallio is some 15,000 people per square kilometre. According to the classic of urban research, Louis Wirth[40] density, I addition to size and diversity, is a crucial

---

38   HS 20.03.2005, D8 Kalliosta ei vieläkään päästä, Tomi Ervamaa.
39   [http://www.kaupunginosat.net/kallio/sivut/kalliokehys.htm] 1.3.2006.
40   Wirth 1938.

denominator of a city. On a European scale Kallio fulfils at least this criterion well.[41]

Because of its small apartments Kallio proves an interesting place for young people to make their first home. The size of the flats in the area, the large number of them and the prices for renting or owner-occupying make it possible for the young and unattached population and for couples with no children to move there. Although by national standards the prices might be considered high, compared to downtown Helsinki it is cheaper to rent or buy a home in Kallio. Since there are no modern homes for families in Kallio, it is no wonder that families with children are moving out: there as simply no homes available that meet modern expectations. When couples get together and children are born it is typical to look for a bigger place and likely a different type of milieu in the suburbs or beyond the city limits of Helsinki.[42]

Indeed, Kallio is characterised by a large amount of mobility. Typically people move in as young adults at the beginning of their studies or working career, live there for a few years then pursue their housing careers elsewhere. Thus Kallio is a sort of jumping off point for young adults, where they have their first encounters with life in urban downtown.[43] From the perspective of the parish Kallio is a sort of a short encounter parish.

One major thing about Kallio is that it takes in large numbers of people from outside Helsinki metropolitan area and then passes them along to other parts of Helsinki and the municipalities of the metropolitan area. What is going on here? One might claim that to a certain extent Kallio makes the urban dweller, living in Kallio urbanises those who move there. Or those moving in must in any case build up a relationship with Kallio and the urban milieu. Many of those moving specifically to Kallio have for the first time to build up their own relation to the city and to their own lives, their own route, their own fixed points, their own social milieu.[44]

---

41   Cantell 2006, 15–16.
42   Cantell 2006, 16.
43   Cantell 2006, 19.
44   Cantell 2006, 15–16.

What kind of urban milieu do young adults find when they move into Kallio? There was appreciation for the pulse of Kallio, its people, and the low entry threshold once they had arrived there.

It feels good to live in Kallio, because there are a lot of people of my age, so it's never been easier to make new friends. And then there are all sorts of cultural experiences, which I like: a lot of music and all that. For that Kallio is a great place to live. Really good in that way and there's action, so I like it. I don't need my own car, everything is within walking distance.

...it's got a bit of a reputation for bragging, but you can get on OK with people. And the people are nice, so that, when I moved in the people living in the building came to carry in my stuff – welcome! [...] It's got a spirit all of its own, you can talk to everybody and the people bale you out if you need it.

Richard Florida, professor of regional geography, in his work *Rise of the Creative Class* has described diverse and open areas like Kallio as creative ecosystems. A creative ecosystem may concern arts and culture, night life, musical circles, restaurants, painters and sculptors, inventors, entrepreneurs, reasonably priced premises, lively city neighbourhoods, animation, education, intimacy, public spaces and third places The third places mentioned in creative ecosystems are not the home or the place of work; these are the two first places. Third places are meeting places such as bars, bookshops and coffee houses where people strangers to each other can talk openly. When family and job as places in life providing interaction and stability in life are nowadays less and less certain and unreliable, and it is still more likely that people live alone and frequently change jobs, third places fill a vacuum.[45] For Florida the sign of a creative ecosystem is that there is an atmosphere of tolerance in the area where homosexuals, lesbians, immigrants and bohemians feel good. The class which Florida speaks of as the creative class also feel good in creative ecosystems. In this class Florida includes various researchers, engineers, painters, musicians, sculptors and knowledge work professionals. According to Florida the number

---

45   Florida 2005, 339.

of people doing creative work has grown enormously in the last twenty years or so, and the ethos of the creative class is in an increasingly prominent place in people's attitudes and choices.[46]

Many young people felt that spiritually they belonged in Kallio. The Church was considered to be a community different from the city. The young people felt that they were spiritually remote from it. *Timo Cantell* has contemplated young Kallio adults and their remoteness from urban milieu and the Church. He compares the situation to the observations of *Simmel*[47] of foreigners, including immigrants and internal migrants, who are physically close but spiritually remote. According to Cantell it is just such a situation which shows that in Kallio young adults are concretely close at hand, living exceptionally close together in the urban Kallio milieu, and yet they appear to be difficult for the Church to access.[48]

Values of young urban adults

Despite wanting to postpone starting a family, family is greatly appreciated among urban young adults. When estimates on the importance of 12 matters were elicited (friends and acquaintances, family, leisure, music, work, exercise and sport, travel, culture and art, studies, popular culture, exerting influence in society, faith/religion) the young adults of Kallio reported that they valued most highly family, and also friends and acquaintances. The average support for both of these was 4.5 (on a scale from 1 "not at

---

46   Florida 2005, 18. According to Florida the so-called creative class navigates towards environments which offer these stimulating and new sensations. According to Florida the environment affects creativity – artistic, cultural, technological and economic – likewise the commercial innovations and afflu-ence to be obtained from it. Florida deems the creative class the new engine of economy. According to Florida's research Finland is a model country of creative economy and ethos. 30 per cent of the Finnish workforce belong to what Florida calls the creative class, and the creativity of the Finnish economy was ranked third by Florida immediately after Sweden and the USA. In these rankings Helsinki proved a creative concentration on the increase. Grünstein 2005, 16.

47   Simmel 2005.

48   Cantell 2006, 21–22.

all important" to 5 "extremely important"). In addition to the foregoing, leisure was also considered extremely important. Least important was religion. (See Figure 4.)

Figure 4. Importance of certain matters as reported by young adults in Kallio (N=500). Means on scale 1-5 (1="not at all important" to 5="extremely important").

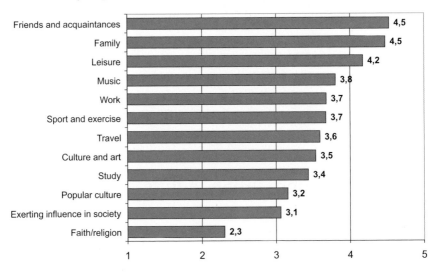

Other Finns are on the same line regarding where the core of a good life is.[49] According, among others, to the European Social Survey at the turn of 2002 and 2003, in a data sample gathered from 22 different countries, Finns over the age of 15 most commonly considered family to be the most important thing among various areas of life. Thereafter came friends (37%) and leisure (25%). Religion, voluntary organisations and politics were the least appreciated areas of life among Finns.[50] According to national surveys family life and its human relations are most commonly considered also to be extremely important for a happy life. The least mentioned by Finns as preconditions for a happy life

---

49   Pohjanheimo 2005, 245–246; Puohiniemi 1993, 28; 2002; Mikkola 2003.
50   Work (18%), religion (8%), voluntary organisations (3%) and politics (1%) were seldom considered extremely important.

were good position and social prestige, societal participation and opportunities to exert influence, good income and high standard of living and spirituality and relationship to God.[51]

No difference was seen between the importance attached to close human relationships by young urban adults and other Finns, but what is the situation with respect to fundamental values? In addition to close human relationships, such fundamental values as one's own health, peace of mind and spiritual harmony the survey on values did not show discrepancies by age. Many other differences in attitudes in the population can be understood through lifespan and period of life. It is entirely natural that younger people should consider working life and success in working life to be more important than do older people. A career and material affluence are more important to those who lack them and for those who have already achieved them or for whom they are things of the past. Indeed, the slick classifications ('bold risk-takers' and 'steady plodders' etc.) are frequently trivially based on age.[52] Growing older increases the appreciation of stability, security and conservation. Then values stressing hedonistic pleasure and enjoyment of life are accorded less importance.[53] Although every generation, on ageing, turns somewhat towards security, uniformity and traditions referred to as conservation, the most recent research findings show that Finns' openness to change has increased from one generation to the next, which has been influenced by a rise in the level of education among other things. Linked to openness to change, enjoyment of life, attaining feeling of pleasure, independence, the opportunity to make one's own choices, creativity and variation and excitement appeal more to Finns than before.[54]

---

51 The most recent national survey of values and attitudes of the Finnish Business and Policy Forum (EVA) also showed that many (83%) Finns consider family life and its human relationships an extremely important precondition for a happy life. After this came good health (77%), good human relationships and friendship (55%) and experiences of love (58%). Torvi & Kiljunen 2005, 58–59.

52 Haikonen & Kiljunen 2003, 341–342.

53 Pohjanheimo 2005, 247; Puohiniemi 2002, 71.

54 Puohiniemi 2002, 71; see also Mikkola 2003.

A farewell to boredom

The openness to change and expansion among young urban adults was also apparent in the instrument in the telephone conversations. There the young adults could be ranked on the RISC three-dimensional socio-cultural field (see Figure 5).[55] The three dimensions (axes) are as follows: Axis 1 (x-axis) expansion – stability, Axis 2 (y-axis) responsibility – enjoyment, Axis 3 (z-axis) flexibility – structure.[56] Parish employees were also ranked on the same attitudinal chart.

When Church employees and young adults are ranked on the same attitudinal chart, it is obvious that Church employees differ quite a lot from the average population. The examination of the attitudes of Church employees can in no way be said to represent the average. Church employees are exceptionally oriented to stability and responsibility. Two out of three Church employees are ranked closer to the stability end of the scale than to the expansion end of the scale. Thus these employees are more loyal to tradition than the average Finn, they opt for a stable situation and do not favour change. Young adults, on the other hand are ranked more markedly than the average Finn towards the extremity of expansion and change.

On the responsibility–enjoyment axis the great majority of Church employees is ranked closer to responsibility, with only approximately every tenth employee being ranked closer to the enjoyment extremity than is the average Finn. All in all the parish employees have thus more appreciation for traditional values and are more conscious of responsibility and less oriented towards change and enjoyment. The young people, for their part differ from the mainstream population in the very opposite direction.

---

55 The instrument used originated in the MiniRISC Study by which respondents can be located on an attitude map. A similar instrument was used in a study on parish employees. See Niemelä 2004, 116–119.

56 RISC Monitor Perusraportti 2002, 6.

Figure 5. The RISC [57]quartiles.[58]

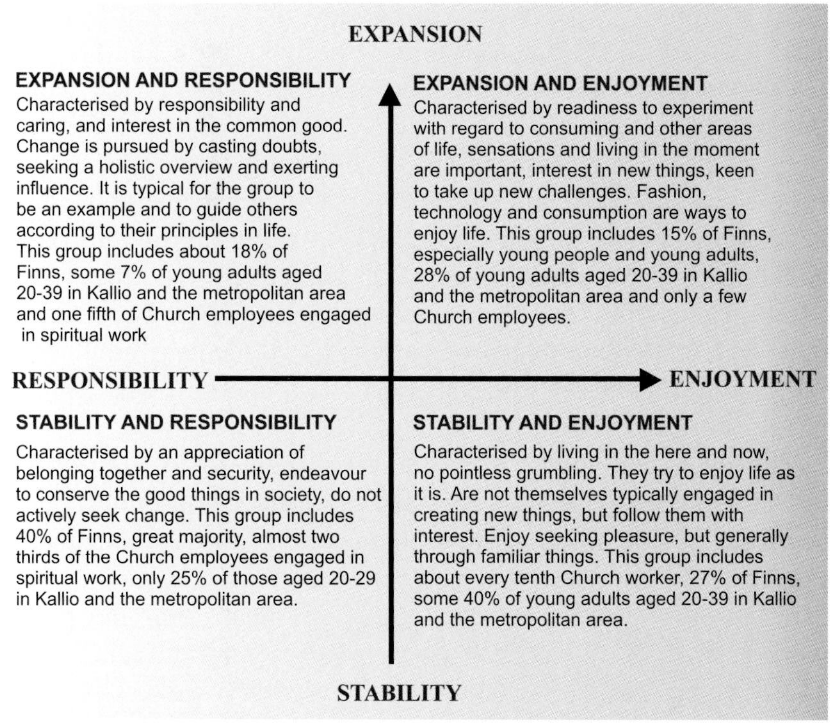

EXPANSION

EXPANSION AND RESPONSIBILITY
Characterised by responsibility and
caring, and interest in the common good.
Change is pursued by casting doubts,
seeking a holistic overview and exerting
influence. It is typical for the group to
be an example and to guide others
according to their principles in life.
This group includes about 18% of
Finns, some 7% of young adults aged
20-39 in Kallio and the metropolitan area
and one fifth of Church employees engaged
in spiritual work

EXPANSION AND ENJOYMENT
Characterised by readiness to experiment
with regard to consuming and other areas
of life, sensations and living in the moment
are important, interest in new things, keen
to take up new challenges. Fashion,
technology and consumption are ways to
enjoy life. This group includes 15% of Finns,
especially young people and young adults,
28% of young adults aged 20-39 in Kallio
and the metropolitan area and only a few
Church employees.

RESPONSIBILITY ————————————————➤ ENJOYMENT

STABILITY AND RESPONSIBILITY
Characterised by an appreciation of
belonging together and security, endeavour
to conserve the good things in society, do not
actively seek change. This group includes
40% of Finns, great majority, almost two
thirds of the Church employees engaged in
spiritual work, only 25% of those aged 20-29
in Kallio and the metropolitan area.

STABILITY AND ENJOYMENT
Characterised by living in the here and now,
no pointless grumbling. They try to enjoy life as
it is. Are not themselves typically engaged in
creating new things, but follow them with
interest. Enjoy seeking pleasure, but generally
through familiar things. This group includes
about every tenth Church worker, 27% of Finns,
some 40% of young adults aged 20-39 in Kallio
and the metropolitan area.

STABILITY

Young adults can be divided into groups more exactly. Then the
young adults of Kallio are characterised by attitudes with a
preference for change and enjoyment. Most generally their
orientation can be described as *multitasking*. What is emphasised
in the attitudes of such multifaceted actors is freedom, adaptation,

57 This attitude is more common among "older" young adults: 25% of those aged
20–29 and 43% of those aged 30–39 in the metropolitan area belong to this
group.
58 RISC Monitor perusraportti 2002; Niemelä 2004; Niemelä 2006b. On the basis
of two dimensions on the RISC socio-cultural map (responsibility-enjoyment
and expansion-stability) people can be classified into four types. Young adults,
especially those under 30 years old, are classified more frequently than other
Finns in the "expansion & enjoyment" and "stability & enjoyment" groups,
Church employees correspondingly into the "stability & responsibility" and
"expansion & responsibility"groups. Of the parish employees engaged in spiritual work two thirds fall into the "stability & responsibity" group.

practicality, self-assurance, competition and being carefree. Their way of life can be summed up in the following motto "Work hard and play hard". Almost one third (30%) of young Kallio adults aged 20–29 are characterised by this attitude to life. Correspondingly only six per cent of parish workers fell within this attitudinal group.

The *fast-moving* characteristic of the young adults was also far from the attitudes of the parish workers: being energetic, fast, networking, ethics to suit the occasion, new opportunities, risks and breaking boundaries was also characteristic of the young adults. Their attitudes can be summed up as "What fun shall we have today?" More than every tenth (16%) young adult aged 20–29 could be described as such an actor, and only one tenth of parish workers.

However, the young Kallio adult is more often a *caretaker* (19%) than fast-moving. The former attitude subsumes being sensible, having responsibility, being co-operative, empathetic, practical, showing solidarity and being cautious. The motto of the caretaker type is "We're all in the same boat". For the parish workers this was by far the most common overall attitude (46%). The next most common attitude among parish workers is *being satisfied,* emphasising thinking along the lines that "there's no home like your own home". Being together, being cautious, religiosity, habits and customs, the small pleasures of life, home and everyday routine and predictability are then the attitudes to life emphasised. Responsibility and permanence are all in all appreciated among parish workers.

As they grow older, the multitasking and fast-moving young adults far from the parish workers may come closer to them – they may reduce speed and their carefree nature may change. It could be observed among the attitudes in Kallio among other things that the older young adults (30–39 years) where typically *caretakers* (25%) and *multitasking* (24%).

Comparison between the values of the Church employees and the young adults shows that it would not be surprising if a young person oriented towards expansion and enjoyment were to have difficulty in finding understanding and interface for his/hers thinking within the Church. The values of the average worker include communal responsibility, stability and tradition – in other words, in the eyes of the young adult likely being set in one's ways, dull and old-fashioned. Young people and young adults are especially far from such values. Typical young people want change, lots of stimuli and action. Most young people and young adults represent such orientation to change and enjoyment which is extremely rare within Church circles.

When the values of young adults in Kallio were compared to those of other young adults in the metropolitan area it emerged that compared to the rest of the metropolitan area young people in Kallio have an appreciation of self-fulfilment, travel, culture and art. Self-fulfilment in hobbies was not mere pleasure-seeking. In hobbies it was considered important that they should entail discussion and time spent with like-minded people. In the choice of hobby was it important for everyone that there should be an opportunity to develop and learn something new. The young people have built up communities to which they belong "with all their hearts".

The most important things in life, are, well, empathy and commu-nication and the quest for approval. This is interesting if there are like three points, so that in a way if you start out from that, that there's communication and discussion then it progresses so you can accept then that leads so that there's empathy. They come to mind just now that they'd be the three mainstays of life.[59]

The young adults in Kallio also had a greater appreciation of going to restaurants and bars. These findings served to strengthen the impression of Kallio as a neighbourhood oriented to entertainment and artistic tastes. The appreciation of studying was likewise greater in Kallio than outside the capital, which likely suggests that Kallio is a typical student neighbourhood. All in all Kallio the values typifying young Kallio adults could be described as modern and indicative of a creative ethos. They can also be described as urban values. Spreading urban values have proven to be the opportunity to enjoy culture and arts and the opportunity to travel and get to know different countries and cultures. Such matters are

---

59   Kumpulainen & Gothoni 2006, 256–257.

stressed more by the inhabitants of large conurbations than by the inhabitants of small municipalities. Likewise the spiritual values in large centres are of less significance than in small centres. In large cities people are more environment friendly and have fewer reservations about foreigners than in small places.[60]

Self-fulfilment is not egoism

The young adults find that societal and religious areas of life are remote and appreciate self-fulfilment, leisure and enjoyment; but they are not narcissistic egoists. What is most important to the young adults of Kallio as to other young adults is close human relationships, family, friends and acquaintances. The same was observed among Scandinavians born in the mid 1980s: Finns, Norwegians, Swedes and Danes. This age group has been called the MeWe generation as it is composed of individualists who also appreciate family and other close human relationships. They are individualists, but not selfish egoists. The existence of collective goals of the young generation is evidenced by its preoccupation with and work for the well-being of the environment. Nature was also ranked high among the young Kallio adults' values, which might seem surprising since there is no nature present anywhere in Kallio. This is no Me-only Generation, or a solely a collective We-only Generation, but a combination of these, MeWe.[61] Thus this is no MeMe culture; there is an endeavour to reconcile one's own interests and those of other people and the environment.[62] Both the Finnish and the Scandinavian findings show that this ethos is more characteristic of women than of men.

The European Social Survey mentioned earlier elicited not only the appreciation of different areas of life but also other values of Finns. The findings show that at the top are trusting human relationships, equality among people, caring for nature and the

---

60 Haikonen & Kiljunen 2003, 359–361, 403–404; Mikkola 2006, 38.

61 Lindgren, Fürth & Lüthi 2005.

62 A similar attitudinal trend also surfaces in Finland in the 1980s among the older age groups when the new urban middle class was studied. Mikkola 2003.

environment, understanding different people and the opportunity to make one's own decisions and to be free. Conversely wealth, prestige, the quest for adventure, success and power are not at all important to Finns. In their values Finns follow the same lines as the French, whose values are closest in Europe to those of Finns. Both Finnish and French women moreover agree that success, wealth and prestige are not at all important – on the other hand equal treatment and taking care of one another and the environment are important.[63]

The values claimed to be typical of the Finns and the French are of the type which the American social scientist Ronald Inglehart has called postmaterial and postmodern. Inglehart has spoken of the spread of these values as a change in world view. It is Inglehart's main tenet that the pursuit of non-material values has grown in relation to the support for materialistic values, which he deems to be part of a more widespread change in which values change alongside the structural changes in society. This extensive ongoing change he calls postmodernisation, stressing the difference of values in an agrarian (traditional) and industrial (modern) and postindustrial (postmodern) society. The change becomes a change in societal aims, authority and in the values of individuals. In the agrarian society the aim was survival. In the industrial society the aim was the maximisation of economic growth. In the postmodern society the aim is the maximisation of subjective well-being. Authorities vary from one form of society to another in such a way that in the agrarian society the dominant authority was that of tradition. In the industrial society it can be described as secular-rational. In the postmodern society the position of authorities can be described such that both the earlier dominant forms of authority are being dismantled. In the agrarian society it was religious and communal norms which coloured individual values. In the industrial society achievement was paramount. In the postindustrial society, according to Inglehart, the values are postmaterialistic and postmodern. In postmodern views the emphasis is on the increasing support for values of

---

63 See the comments by the professor of statistics, Seppo Laaksonen, in the newpaper *Helsingin Sanomat* on 29 November 2004.

freedom – freedom of the individual, self-directedness and openmindedness. By postmaterialistic values Inglehart is referring to non-materialistic values – of self appreciation, social relations and self fulfilment. This value orientation stressing quality of life is also linked to support for environment values.[64]

Figure 6. Location of different countries on the value map by Inglehart.[65]

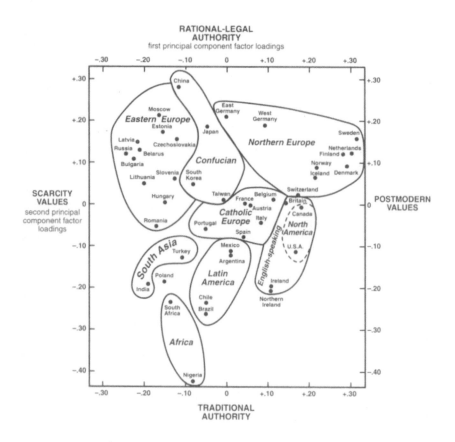

In Inglehart's worldwide examination the Nordic countries have been the forerunners in the changes in values. Indeed, on the one hand Finland has gone far in the creation of an information society

---

64   Inglehart 1997, 67–107, 267–292; Inglehart & Baker 2000.
65   Inglehart 1997, 349. See also Inglehart & Baker 2000; Inglehart 2003.

based on wireless communication and on the other hand represents, with the other Nordic countries, a cultural basis which has been found to offer a fertile soil for the propagation of new kinds of values. Finland is in the vanguard of many changes. According to Inglehart's measurements it is not the United States of America which is at the forefront of change; if we are to name pioneering countries, such are the economically prosperous Nordic countries coloured by the Protestant tradition. The long cherished notion of the Americanisation of the world does not today appear to be well founded.[66] The ranking of Finland and the other Nordic countries in Inglehart's global comparison is presented in the Figure 6.

On the map the Nordic countries are close to other Protestant countries in the north of Europe. The spread of novel values especially to the Nordic countries has been claimed to be due not only to economic and physical stability, but also to the fact that the Nordic cultural tradition is conducive to the spread of values.[67] In the Protestant Nordic countries already advocating individualism, there is fertile soil for the spread and propagation of new values. The spread of new values is likely connected to the Protestant "spirit of free examination". According to Durkheim free self scrutiny is not due to its desirability *per se,* as it contains as much sorrow as it does joy, but to the fact the people need this freedom. There is only one reason for this need; the wavering of traditional beliefs. According to Durkheim the great freedom for individual thought allowed by Protestantism is due to the small amount of shared beliefs and habits of people within its sphere.[68] "If their strength were still the same, it would never occur to people to criticise them. If they still had the same authority, people would not demand the right to verify these sources of authority".[69] Thinking only develops out of the necessity of filling the gap which occurs, which it, however, has not itself created. Thinking emerges only when established beliefs run into a state of

---

66   Inglehart & Baker 2000, 49; Inglehart 1997, 22.

67   Inglehart & Baker 2000.

68   Durkheim 1985, 174–175.

69   Durkheim 1985, 174.

dissolution.[70] The Figure 6 also shows that Finland is not ranked among the extremely individualistic countries. Finns, as noted, appreciate the not only values stressing the freedom of the individual but also consideration for others.

The conception of the American sociologist Daniel Yankelovich of changes in values after the Second World War corresponds with that of Inglehart. In his research Yankelovich has observed that the generations born after the Second World War are less often given to considering going forward in life having various external manifestations: economic well-being, high social position and life in the traditional framework of family life. In place of the pursuit of the traditional measures of financial security and success measures, people have begun to consider life more a matter of self-fulfilment, where more value than before is attached to one's own inner world, examination of one's own needs and their fulfilment. This is connected to stressing the importance of experiences. Yankelovich has considered greater openmindedness to be a precondition for the spread of self-fulfilment. Increased openmindedness and the decline of traditional moral conceptions and matters serving to broaden the space of the variety of choices have rendered self-fulfilment a possible option in more and more different areas of life.[71]

The ethos of the creative class evinced by Florida is very similar to the novel values described above. A very similar trend in values has also been found by the sociologist Paul H. Ray and the psychologist Ruth Anderson in their research on creative cultural persons. Creative cultural persons in their research were generally active in society in matters affecting themselves, were keen to protect the environment and in favour of gender equality. Many of them were religiously inclined, although they did not support any religious mainstream. They were also more likely than others to be interested in self development and in human relations. They also had selective tastes and enjoyed exotic experiences. In their own opinion they were not materialists in the economic sense.[72]

---

70   Durkheim 1985, 174–175.
71   Yankelovich 1994, 38; Yankelovich et al. 1985, 33–34; Yankelovich 1981.
72   Ray & Anderson 2000; Florida 2005, 143-144.

Enter authenticity

The ethos of the new generation is not only the spread of individualism considered characteristic of the present time, i.e. the greater appreciation of the freedom of the individual and self-directedness and the individual's greater independence of traditions and societal and religious institutions, but also the pursuit of a certain way of being. Among the young urban adults interviewed there was a great deal of talk about "my thing" and its pursuit, "what I really want". On this basis the choice of hobbies and involvement in many other kinds of activity and actions were considered. If the activity felt like "something for me" there was reason to continue with it. In opposite cases continuing was called into question. From the perspective of Church membership this became apparent in claims to the effect that the traditional Church was not "my thing". Subjectification and seeking a foothold for identity from one's self thus appeared concretely. The young adults'self scrutiny and weighing up of things led them to a solution, what feels most appropriate to oneself and to support the self. The attitude can be dubbed *authenticity*.[73]

In authenticity what is essential is that in forming his/her values and in his/her other activities, the individual is consciously and deliberately true to him/herself, not slavishly adhering to habits and authorities outside him/herself.[74] Although in authenticity such value consideration is essential, it does not prevent one from arriving at more generally held values and meanings. The individual can be said to be authentic when s/he has been able to exert influence on the formation of his/her conceptions, values and activities and has employed personal consideration in their formation the basis of which is the scrutiny of his/her own genuine

---

73 Taylor 1995. It is just this demand for authenticity which has been considered a change feature in our time, discriminating between past and present. E.g. Ferrara 1998, 5; Taylor 1995, 55. Authenticity would be just like a mature stage in the triumphant progress of individualism, individualism at its most perfect.

74 Taylor 1995, 57–59. See also Pietarinen 1994.

needs, desires and hopes.[75] The individual is then his/her own norm, and the ultimate authority for that assessment or action is not some external force such as religious authority (e.g. tradition, holy scriptures or other teachings), secular legislation, general or peer opinion, political ideology, science or the teachings of one's forefathers. Then a modern person can typically live in a manner classified as traditional: s/he may belong to the Church, attach great importance to family life, do a great deal of work etc. What is essential is that people arrive at their solutions on a voluntary basis through conscious self scrutiny.

Thus the way of thinking of the new generation would not appear to show whether a person supports such attitudes, values, beliefs and behaviours which have typically been classified as modern, but rather how people arrive at different solutions in their lives. Modernity is no ethos or ideology, but rather an attitude to life in which people are open to innovations, freely assess the various alternatives and arrive at solutions which best suit oneself and support one's own real self.

Religion can be deemed a modern solution when, instead of certainties imparted in the community, we have the results of individually made choices. A religious choice emanating from the self and which follows its own true "self" is modern. Generally such a solution differs from the mainstream of institutional religiousness, and from the world of Christianity to which many of us are joined at baptism and to which we are generally socialised in our educational institutions. This is because, like other modernity, religious modernity requires that the old be called into question. Modern religiousness is "achieved" personally in a world of many kinds of options; it is not given.

The spread of the ideal of authenticity means that the individual's subjective reality has become the object of ultimate interest. At the same time the religious and many other mainstream institutions have increasingly ceased to be a safe haven for the self. Rather than being "home", they have begun to be considered realities which stifle the self, which distort and alienate the self.[76]

---

75   See also Pietarinen 1994, 22–23.
76   Berger et al. 1977, 74–77, 86.

Compared to the lives of earlier generations the new generations pay more attention to their own selves, turning in on themselves and building their lives on themselves.

In referring to the way of thinking of the new generation we do not refer to an ethos or ideology, but to an attitude to life in which people are open to innovation and desirous of remaining faithful to one's own true self. In this way it is not so harsh or firm as to relinquish all that is deemed traditional. It is literally porous. The traditional and the novel co-exist in the individual's thinking. This is manifest in an increase in all kinds of hybrids and third "options".[77] Today, too, religion can be called a "miscellany", and it cannot be described as a waxing or waning of Church religion or secularity.

---

[77] Mikkola 2003, 267, 303.

III RELIGIOSITY OF THE NEW GENERATION

Religious commitment is especially characteristic of certain population groups in Finland: pensioners, rural residents and women appear to be more religious than the average person. Similarly, a few "weak links" can be found with regard to religious attitudes: especially young people and the Helsinki metropolitan area. According to the findings these groups in Finland are less religious according to all the traditional ways of measuring religiosity: among other things they are more passive than other groups about participating in religious observances, they pray or read religious literature or otherwise practice their religion privately less frequently. Belief in the traditional Christian tenets is also less than in other population groups.[1] In adulthood faith increases linearly the older the age group. The older the age group the more important is the role of religion and the Church in their lives, and the more faithful the people are to the Church and its traditional conceptions of religion and world of values. The difference in religiosity of different age groups and its linear pattern can be seen in Figure 7, examining the share of those who believe in God among the different age groups. The figure shows the same trend whatever dimension of religiosity is examined. On the other hand the same "less religiosity" can be observed in many studies if residents of the metropolitan area are compared to those resident elsewhere in Finland.[2] Residents of the metropolitan area are less religious in a traditional sense than those living elsewhere.

---

1   See e.g. Kääriäinen & Niemelä & Ketola 2003.
2   See e.g. Kääriäinen & Niemelä & Ketola 2003, 203–209.

Figure 7. Share of those in the different age groups who believe in God. (The Church Monitor 2004.) N=2 555. %.

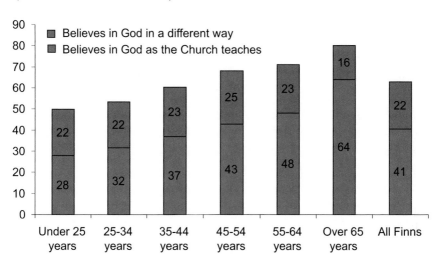

Why are young people less religious in a traditional sense? Differences between old and young are not new: as long as there has been research data available older people have been more religious than younger people. These differences have traditionally been explained in three different ways: the traditional model focuses on the development processes associated with the respective stages of life.[3] Then the increase in religiosity occurring with increasing age is explained by the fact that it is an outcome of the development tasks accompanying ageing. The alternative life span model attributes differences in ages to changes in social roles and not to development processes associated with different stages of life.[4] Here the changes in religiosity occurring with age are attributed to changes occurring in the individual's role, especially in the family role. Then the main factors with bearing on religiosity are deemed to be having children and parenthood or the death of one's own parents. The third explanatory model attributes difference in religiosity among people of different ages to cohort effects; in different ages it is different to live and grow, and external factors have different effects on different generations.

---

3   Bahr 1970.
4   E.g. Chaves 1991.

This is the explanatory model which has caused most disagreement among researchers, and particularly with regard to the influence of secularisation. But to what extent is the observed decrease in religiosity among Finnish young people and young adults a consequence of the influence of a given age and especially of secularisation and to what extent is it simply a case of being younger?

Studies on the religiosity of Finns show, as might be expected, that religiosity does indeed have a slight tendency to increase with age: the generation which while still of working age has at least so far become religiously active as pensioners.[5] Those around the age of 50 in the 1980's prayed more actively some twenty years later when approaching retirement age. There are also more of those who believe in God and who could not imagine resigning from the Church. It is only attendance at services which has not increased. A corresponding increase in religiosity is also apparent in all other age groups: The private practice of religion increases with age likewise the significance of belonging to the Church, even though there is no increase in attendance at services or other religious participation.

Thus the optimists of the Church may console themselves that young adults have always been less religious but will duly become more so as they grow older and that they can therefore stop reading this book here and now. However, the research shows that there are also cohort differences in religiosity. Today's young people are less religious than young people a few decades ago. Comparison of the religiosity of different groups over a period of twenty years shows that the differences between age groups now apparent are not only a consequence of differences developing with age, but to some extent also of differences between eras and also to some extent of secularisation – or at least of a change in religiosity. The young people of today, like those of working age and those who have retired are, from the perspective of religiosity, also less religious and less committed to the Church and its conceptions of faith than those of the same age twenty years earlier. This change is most pronounced among citydwellers.

---

5   See Kääriäinen & Niemelä & Ketola 2003, 198–202.

The change brought by the passage of time is very obvious among young people and young adults. It is also obvious with regard to churchgoing. The share of passive churchgoers and of those who never go to church has increased among young people and young adults. There has also been a decrease in the number of churchgoers among those of working age. On the other hand, from the perspective of private practice of religion, such as praying, the differences are small or non-existent in all age groups.[6]

There is a strong link between the foregoing and the change otherwise occurring in Finns' religiosity in recent decades. In light of the changes in recent decades, Finns' religiosity is characterised by the weakened position of religious institutions. This is seen first and foremost in people's decreased membership of religious bodies, as also in a reduction in the clear commitment among Finns to the teachings of the Church and in participation in traditional forms of religion.[7] These changes are apparent in all age groups. However, at the same time activity in praying has remained the same. Nor has there in recent decades been any decline in the belief in the existence of God or some supernatural force. Likewise the share of Finns who believe that God is important in their lives and who derive help from religion has remained the same. However, at the same time, the share of those who believe in the traditional teachings of the Church has declined.[8] Thus this is not a matter of one-way secularisation – hardly anyone believes that.[9] Rather, religion has become increasingly private. While the religious institutions have become weaker, this has not led to an overall decline of religion. Among the young urban population especially, the new middle class, commitment to the forms of traditional religion has proven to be slight.[10]

The wider youth of the city have become a new kind of middle class. In modernisation the middle class has been a group which

6   Kääriäinen & Niemelä & Ketola 2003, 198–202.
7   See Kääriäinen & Niemelä & Ketola 2005, 82, 112–113.
8   See Kääriäinen & Niemelä & Ketola 2005.
9   See Davie 2000; Davie 2006; Casanova 1994.
10   Mikkola 2003.

assimilates novelties first and passes them on to others, and the receptiveness to new things is not confined to the material world, but also extends to cultural trends in general. Thus it makes sense to examine the Kallio people also as an ethical and religious core and even as a group of forerunners. The young adults of Kallio represent a section of the population which moves and consumes most actively if consumption is taken to mean spending time in city spaces and reception of the cultural offering. The young urban active population has become the primary target of media and market. It is to them that the first novelty products are marketed and assumed to spread through them to the rest of the population. Such a dissemination of ethos via this "new middle class" to the rest of the population will also most likely occur in the religious field. The phenomena first observed among the young urban population will slowly filter through to the rest of the population.[11] That being so, the present appearance of the religiosity of that section of the population can probably be taken as an indication of the development about to take place in the rest of the population.

As a neighbourhood, the Kallio district constitutes an ideal testbed on which to examine the dissemination of new values and ways of life, because there are a great number of young adults in Kallio. It is also a good place in which to research young adults because it is a prime example of the phenomenon which has been referred to as the postponement of adulthood, the prolongation of youth. Almost all those aged 20–29 in Kallio have no families, likewise those aged 30–39. Compared to the rest of the metropolitan area there are in Helsinki, and especially in Kallio, more of those who by the age of thirty have not had children. Thus the urban way of life and today's special features show up particularly well when researching the young adults of Kallio.

An urban environment cannot of itself be considered fundamentally unchristian or unreligious, but there are features of the urban lifestyle which do not support traditional forms of religiosity. There is indeed a connection between the long-term alienation from the Church and urbanisation, but other phenomena

---

11   Mäenpää 206, 353–357.

of social change also belong in the same period of time. Those changes in ideals, such as focus on the individual and the spread of the ideal of authenticity are a challenge to institutional religion. The development in information technology and the growth of mass entertainment serve to make society more liberal and have pluralistic values. People are more aware of the various alternative ways of living and different alternatives are available to more and more people. In many ways, we live in a society of plenty. One might conjecture that drifting away from the Church progresses at the same rate as the boredom of youth.

Kallio, more urban than the urban, constitutes in its religious attitudes a particularly challenging area for the Church: in many senses. The young adults of Kallio are far removed from the Church and its system of values. The share of those belonging to the Church is smaller than that in the rest of the metropolitan area and in the rest of Finland. (Kallio 65.5%, Helsinki as a whole 68.8%[12], Finland as a whole 83.1% in 2005 and 82.4% in 2006). The relative share of young adults who have resigned from the Church is also at its very highest in Kallio.

Questioning of belonging

The telephone interviews suggest that of all the young adults in Kallio, almost half (48%) were at the edge of being Church members at the time of the interviews – that is, they were either considering resigning from the Church or joining it – or then totally beyond the sphere of the Church.[13] The difference from all Finns is noteworthy. Of all Finns fewer than one third (30%) are outside the Church or on the periphery. The rest of the

---

12 Of the young Kallio adults participating in the telephone interviews 71% belonged to the Evangelical Lutheran Church of Finland, of those interviewed in the Helsinki metropolitan area 78% belonged to the Evangelical Lutheran Church of Finland. Fewer than 2% belonged to the Orthodox Church and in Kallio less than one percent belonged to other religious dominations, the corresponding figure for the rest of the metropolitan area being 3%. The remainder did not belong to any religious domination at all.

13 A total of 18 of these young adults in Kallio who are "on the edge" were interviewed face-to-face.

metropolitan area is situated somewhere in between Kallio and the rest of Finland. Of all young people in the metropolitan area over a third (39%) were either outside the Church or on the edge of membership. The shares of young adults with various attitudes towards the Church membership in Kallio and in the metropolitan area and of all Finns are shown in Table 1.

Table 1. Attitudes towards Church membership among young adults in Kallio and in the Helsinki metropolitan area and among all Finns. (Gallup Ecclesiastica 2003; Telephone Survey Young Adults in Kallio 2004; Telephone Survey Young Adults in the Helsinki Metropolitan Area 2004.) %.

	Young adults in Kallio district (N=499) %	Young adults in Helsinki metropolitan area (N=994) %	All Finns (N=1005) %
INSIDE THE CHURCH	Total 52%	Total 61%	Total 70%
Could not contemplate leaving the Church under any circumstances	11	17	32
Has never considered leaving the Church and does not see it as a likely prospect	24	30	24
Has considered leaving the Church but has always decided against it	17	14	14
ON THE EGDE OF CHURCH MEMBERSHIP	Total 21%	Total 19%	Total 13%
Has frequently considered leaving the Church but has not come to a clear decision	11	10	7
Is likely to leave the Church at some point	8	7	4
Does not belong to the Church and is likely to join the Church at some point.	0.6	1	1
Does not belong to church, but has frequently considered joining the Church but has not come to a clear decision	0.6	1	1
OUTSIDE THE CHURCH	Total 27%	Total 20%	Total 17%
Does not belong to the Church, but has considered joining the Church but has always decided against it	2	3	2
Does not belong to the Church and has never considered joining the Church and does not see it as a likely prospect	8	7	5
Does not belong to the Church and could not contemplate joining the Church under any circumstances	17	10	10
Total	100	100	100

To many of those on the edge or considering resigning one can apply the description by the American Joseph Fischter of parishioners who within the Church are "outsiders" or "dormant". Those who are dormant are those who have drifted away from the parish, whose actions and thinking are no longer regulated by the Church. What connects them to the parish is their baptism or possibly some other Church rite. They may also have their own children baptised, but that is as far as contact goes. According to Fischter their moving completely out of the Church is only a short step as they are already "outsiders" inside.[14] Among the youth of the metropolitan area there are more such "dormant" and "outsiders inside the Church" and also of those completely outside the Church than there are among Finns as a whole. In addition, one fifth of young adults in Kallio did not belong to the Church at all.

Once an individual has moved outside the Church, there is generally no returning to it. More than half (54%) of the young Kallio adults who had left the Church could not imagine themselves rejoining it under any circumstances, one third (32%) had not even thought about it. Only approximately every tenth (14%) of those resigning from the Church deemed it possible to rejoin. The notion of rejoining the Church was more remote from women who had resigned from it than men. Notably among those of the younger age group (20–29 years) who had resigned from the Church women could in no way imagine that they would rejoin.[15] For at least the last ten years this youngest age group has been the largest among those resigning from the Church in the Helsinki parishes.[16] According to the Kallio telephone interview data there are also more of those in the youngest age group who have never

---

14   Fischter 1954, 68–79; see also Sihvo 1979, 41–42.

15   Over two thirds (71%) of women living in Kallio and less than half (42%) of men were of the opinion that they could not imagine joining the Church under any circumstances. 92% of women aged 20–29 were of this opinion, and of those aged 30–39 45%. Men were slightly less abrupt in their views (46% of those aged 20–29 and 39% of those aged 30–39). The abrupt attitude among women might in part be due to the fact that at the time of the interviews some male members of the clergy had achieved publicity because of their opposition to the ordination of women.

16   In the last ten years their share of those resigning (18–24-year-olds) has grown by ten percentage points (from 37% in 2004 to 46%).

ever belonged to any religious denomination.[17] Of those who have never belonged to the Church a large majority (71%) could not imagine that they would join the Church under any circumstances.

Membership of the Church as a whole does not have as much meaning for young people and young adults as it does for older generations – this can be seen throughout Finland. Commitment to Church membership increases steadily with age (see Figure 8). Of all 25-year-olds only one out of five could not imagine resigning from the Church. By contrast, as may as two out of three of those aged 65 and over could not imagine resigning from the Church under any circumstances. In Kallio only one out of six of those 20–39-years old could not imagine resigning from the Church. In both Kallio and elsewhere in the metropolitan area about one in four respondents considered resignation. All in all there are very few among the young adults of Kallio who could not imagine leaving the Church in any circumstances.

Figure 8. Commitment to Church membership among Finns of different ages belonging to the Church. (Gallup Ecclesiastica 2003; Telephone Survey Young Adults in Kallio 2004; Telephone Survey Young Adults in the Helsinki Metropolitan Area 2004.) %.

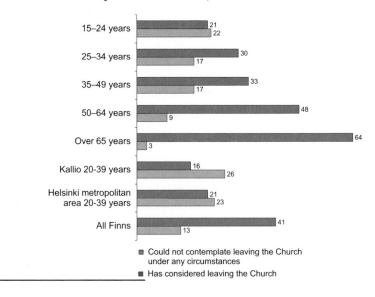

17   9% of those aged 20–29 and 4% of those aged 30–39 have never belonged to any religious organisation.

If the commitment to the Church of all Church members is examined over a longer period of time, there is one change of attitude in particular. Commitment to the Church has been surveyed ever since the 1970s using the questions shown in Table 2. In the light of this questionnaire data over a long period of time, there has been a distinct drop in the number of those who have never pondered their relation to Church membership. There has been a decrease in their number since the mid 1970s of 15 percentage points (from 41 to 26). Thus Church membership would nowadays appear to be more associated with more consideration. There are ever fewer Finnish members of the Church who have never considered leaving the Church, in other words who have never taken a stand on their membership. When scrutinising Table 2 it should be noted that only the attitudes of those belonging to the Church are taken into account. As can be seen in the table, the share of those belonging to the Church has gradually declined throughout the period. Thus there are a few more people every year who are entirely outside the scrutiny and outside membership.

Table 2. Views of members of the Evangelical Lutheran Church of Finland regarding resignation from the Church 1976–2007. %.

Have you ever considered leaving the Church?	Finns					
	1976	1982	1988	1995	2003	2007
Could not contemplate leaving the Church under any circumstances	37	41	42	42	41	41
Has never considered leaving the Church and does not see it as a likely prospect	41	36	31	29	29	26
Has considered leaving the Church but has always decided against it	11	12	13	17	17	17
Has frequently considered leaving the Church but has not come to a clear decision	7	7	9	7	8	12
Is likely to leave the Church at some point	4	3	4	4	5	4
N	1 137	1 025	828	828	827	793
Share of Church members among Finns	92 %	90 %	88 %	86 %	84 %	82 %

The increase in the number of those reflecting on Church membership is a proof of an increase in a questioning mindset. The pioneers of modernisation research, Alex Inkeles and David Smith were in their day of the opinion that contemplation is one characteristic of the modern person. They claimed that it is a precondition for modernisation that a person should be capable of forming opinions and have his/her own views on various issues. This was manifest in the study in a tendency to take a stand on things. A tendency not to take a stand could be called a traditional attitude.[18]

On the one hand the strength of the Evangelical Lutheran Church of Finland and on the other hand the prevailing freedom of religion in the country create the preconditions for the contemplation of Church membership to be something worth contemplating. Within the Church the discussion is frequently confined to mere comments on the number of resignations and the problem is seen to be the Church itself. The solution evinced is to overhaul the activities of the Church, such as renewing the forms of service. Those resigning are frequently seen as secularised egoists characterised by indifference, and who, in pursuit of their own interests, decide not to pay their Church taxes.

Both the survey and interview data show that those resigning from the Church are somewhat focused on themselves. However, it is difficult to consider them selfish egoists. They are, on the other hand, characterised by seeking for real content and meaning. For those resigning from the Evangelical Lutheran Church it is frequently more important than for those who belong to the Church to make their own decisions and to be free. They also want more frequently to be creative and generate new ideas. The importance of making their own decisions and freedom were also stressed among the young Kallio adults interviewed. They had great faith in their own discretion and were greatly alienated from the notion of the Bible and its teachings as a guiding light in life.

If we look at Finland as a whole, on the basis of the membership figures of religious communities, Finland is an

---

18   Inkeles & Smith 1974, 20–21.

exceptionally uniform country. In 2006, 4.3 million Finns belonged to the Evangelical Lutheran Church of Finland. This corresponds to 82.4 per cent of the population. The proportion of the population of the country that belongs to the Evangelical Lutheran Church has, however, gradually decreased. Fifty years ago the proportion was ten percentage points higher. One per cent of Finns belong to Finland's other national church, the Orthodox Church. Only one in a hundred belong to other registered religious organisation. In addition, approximately 1 per cent of Finns belong to unregistered religious denominations, mainly Pentecostal assemblies. Thus in Finland the Evangelical Lutheran Church is not in competition with any denomination in terms of membership, but only with religious non-commitment. Fifteen per cent of Finns do not belong to any registered religion. Their number has gradually risen.

However, for Finns the membership of a religious community does not necessarily mean that a person regards himself or herself as religious. In particular, membership of the Evangelical Lutheran Church is a rather neutral expression of religious belief, as in the other Nordic countries. According to the World Values 2005 survey, 63 per cent of those who belong to the Evangelical Lutheran Church consider themselves religious. The proportion among all Finns is 61 per cent. Women consider themselves more often religious than men. Almost three quarters of women (69%) regard themselves as religious, and half of men (52%).

As in the other Nordic countries, so also in Finland membership of the Evangelical Lutheran Church has been seen as a part of national identity.[19] This attitude to Church membership, however, no longer seems to describe the relation of the new generation to the Church. Unlike their parents, young adults no longer perceive membership of the Evangelical Lutheran Church to be part of the Finnish way of life, and for them being a member of the Church has hardly anything to do with being a good citizen or a good Finn. For the older generations, however, being a member of the Church was an integral part of the Finnish way of life. This perception of

19   See Gustafson & Pettersson 2000; Davie 2000; Sundback 2000.

Church membership as a part of the Finnish way of life is particularly pronounced among those of pension age, of whom half (50%) consider it a very important reason for belonging to the Church. Among those under 25 years old only 11 per cent think in this way. Among those aged 50–64 membership of the Church is still clearly part of the Finnish way of life. The younger the age group, the less important this is. In no other reason for belonging to the Church do the views of the young generation differ so much from those of older generations.[20] Among the older age groups the adage *home, church and fatherland* is deeply ingrained. This connection is the more tenuous the younger the age group is concerned. Among the older age groups Lutheranism would therefore appear to be clearly a characteristic pertaining to the national Finnish identity – a good Finn is also a Lutheran. Lutheranism was also once one of the factors which during the period of Russian domination distinguished Finns from Russians and laid the foundations for a feeling of nationalism. Among young people and young adults Lutheranism no longer appears to have such a significance connected to a feeling of nationalism.[21] This being the case, membership of the Church seems to be more of a personal choice for the young. From this it follows that the threshold for the choice to resign from the Church, for example, if an individual feels unable to commit to its message, is lower than it is for older people.

The study shows that Finns who have resigned from the Church describe themselves less frequently than Church members as the sort of people for whom it is important to maintain tradition and custom. Those who have resigned from the Church also consider themselves to be of the type which believes that it is important to behave properly than those who belong to the Church. It is not important for them to live according to some prevailing models. Those who have resigned from the Church also describe themselves less frequently as people for whom it is important to be

---

20   The difference between the different age groups. F=33,19***. Source Gallup Ecclesiastica 2003. The survey elicited the importance of a total of twenty different reasons for membership

21   Niemelä 2006a, 195–196.

humble and conventional. In the eyes of young urban adults the Evangelical Lutheran Church of Finland frequently seemed to have parted company with the modern world, to be reactionary and intolerant. Many young people felt that they and their values, beliefs and living habits did not fit into such a church. The young Kallio adults interviewed partly blamed the Church for the construction in society of "assumption people" who *"are of a certain appearance, a certain type and fit into certain model"*. The model constructed was deemed old-fashioned, as it was thought that the Church has become *"stuck at the turn of the 1800s and 1900s"* while the values of the rest of society have become more diverse, for example through internationalisation. Young adults were disturbed by the idea that *"there is always that one view on everything and it's an absolute truth in a way – it sees things in black and white"*. Humility was also a feature which those young people far from the Church did not rate highly either as a characteristic of themselves or of the Church. Since the Christianity represented by the Church is seen to be *"horribly humble and devout"*, it is a sorrowful religion, which *"somehow has no appeal whatsoever for me"*. The Church, felt to be an old-fashioned and intolerant institution, did not appear to the internationalised young people with their pluralistic values to be a credible actor in a global world.

Young urban adults can be considered liberal. In politics they consider that their thinking is closest to the agendas of the so-called new political parties – the Greens and the New Left. Compared to the other political parties the Greens and the New Left were considered tolerant urban parties. They were attracted to the greens by *"broadmindedness and plurality of values and on the other hand also shared responsibility, which also includes environmental issues"*. Among other things almost all the interviewees on the edge of Church membership were ideologically inclined towards the Left or the Greens. Those who had resigned from the Church also on the whole supported most often the Greens or the Left Wing Alliance.[22] They were a long way away from conservative thinking. It is commonly said of

22   Niemelä 2006a, 177–179.

conservatism that it is not one single ideological system or ideology, but rather a certain kind of attitude to life, a certain attitude towards societal and political phenomena.[23] Conservatism is not linked to any specific social system: *"It is not a dogmatic ideology, but a political attitude"*.[24] Conservatism is an anti-theoretical trend moulded at any given time or in any given society to suit itself and which does not give instructions for action in different situations. It characteristically emphasises that history and tradition be taken into account in actions. Russel Kirk puts it like this: *"It is not wealth, not power, not sensitivity nor social position that makes a citizen a conservative, but rather a deeply ingrained suspicion of the new and the dubious."*[25] The content of conservatism is frequently taken to be defending national traditions and resisting rapid changes in society. Conservatism becomes involved with patriotism and religion. For many conservatives a return to traditional values is an important theme, which frequently also entails a strong emphasis on family values and religiosity. Conservatism differs from liberalism, which embodies a critical assessment of state power and a general broadmindedness and tolerance.[26] The liberalism of young urban adults is linked to a critical assessment of the Church.

No to institutions

The young people do not perceive institutions as being as important as they were considered by older age groups. For young adults faith is decidedly personal, and many young people do not feel that they need the Church as an institution to strengthen their own faith. Faith pertains to the individual and is a private matter. A distinction is made between faith and institution. Only one out of ten (11%) respondents under 25 years of age considered it an extremely important and one out of five (21%) a fairly important reason for belonging to the Church that the Church

---

23   Nousiainen 1992, 86–87.
24   Rantala 1960, 11.
25   Rantala 1960, 64.
26   Saastamoinen 1998, 9–14, 18–19.

strengthens belief in God. Among pensioners those considering this extremely or fairly important amounted to 72 per cent.[27]

The differences described above do not alone account for the fact that religion is less important to young people than to older people. If we examine the views of only those who believe in God as taught in the Christian religion the pensioners still consider the support of the Church to be more important than do the young people. Such a tenuous connection between religion and institution is also clearly visible in those on either side of age 40. Young adults and those of working age therefore increasingly think that it is just as possible to have faith regardless of the Church institution. People have thus become more aware of their own roles in the formation of their religious lives. Definitions of religious belief and behaviour have become recognisably subjective rather than normative. According to this view a person may be a good Christian even if s/he does not belong to the Church.[28] One interviewee, who has resigned from the Church, reported in a personal interview how for him the ethos had taken shape according to which he neither wanted nor needed *"any pastor or the like to guide and guard me"*. What was important for him was that *"people think for themselves, think things out and live according to that"*. He drifted away from the Church partly because *"you can't criticise the word of God, the message or anything else. [...] I surely don't adhere to that, but I feel that I live and am good to my neighbour so that not even Jesus could think that I'm no damned good even if I don't belong to the Church. Then I think that it's just useless and I find more faults than good things for myself."*

This interviewee cannot be called traditional in his beliefs, even though he describes himself as a religious person. In his own words *"the religious field"* interests him *"but not only the Christian church, that there's good to be found in every religion"*. Nor can his ethical base for life be described as a traditional Protestant work ethic, rather as a bohemian ethic. The Protestant work ethic is usually used to refer to a trend in values in which

---

27   Gallup Ecclesiastica 2003.
28   Cf. Roof 2003, 139.

work is deemed the principle content of life and in which there is emphasis on working hard, conscientiousness, ambition, obedience to authority, capability, parsimony and affluence as a virtue. Conversely idleness, ample leisure, the pursuit of pleasure and spending money are considered vices.[29] The bohemian ethic is more hedonistic. There is appreciation for pleasure, happiness and individuality. Creativity, rebelliousness, self-expression, marked pursuit of sensations and anti-materialism are appreciated. This is not a matter of hoarding enjoyment or reckless living, but rather of tasting and appreciating the small pleasures life offers.[30]

> *...it's surely the basic idea in all those religions, this moaning and then of course for some it's the goal of life after death, but I wouldn't go for that myself. I do try to enjoy my life here and I don't refrain from pleasures just because somebody thinks it's wrong at the time. In my opinion a person always knows deep down inside what is right.*

So why do young people who are critically disposed to institutions want to be members? The research shows that the reasons for being a member of the Church are on the whole very much connected to the phase of life and emanate from the life situation.

The most important reason for young people to belong to the Church is the option to be married in church. This is prominent above all among those under the age of 30. The next important reason for young people is the option for their children to have a Christian baptism. This is prominent before and after age 30. Thus the young adults stress as reasons for being members of the Church those things which in a given stage of life are topical, getting married and the birth of children and the Church rites associated with these. Among older age groups the one reason deemed most important is the option of being buried by the Church.[31] According to various studies for a great number of Church members Church rites are the main single reason for belonging to the Church and for many the only concrete

---

29   See e.g. Furnham 1996, 13–17, 81–86; Weber 1989; see also Mikkola 2003, 80, 179.
30   Florida 2005, 296–297; Brooks 2001; see also Mikkola 2003, 88–89.
31   Niemelä 2006a, 179–186; 194-195.

connection with the parish and the pastor. In the opinion of many who are alienated from the Church, too, rites are the strongest and last tie with the Church.[32]

The Church members were classified using K-means cluster analysis into different groups according to why they belonged to the Church i.e. what issues they consider important for their Church membership.[33] All in all among young adults throughout Finland there are more members than in other age groups who stress Church rites and more for whose Church membership there does not appear to be any reason. In the young age groups there are fewer members who stress the spiritual task of the Church than there are in the older age groups (see Figure 9).[34]

Figure 9. Shares of different types of members in different age groups. (Gallup Ecclesiastica 2003.) %.

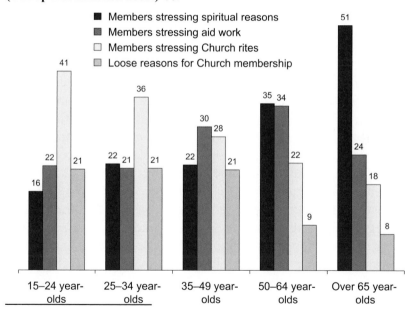

32   Ks. Kirkko muutosten keskellä 2004, 57–58; Sihvo 1992.

33   See Niemelä 2006a, 181–186, 197. The groups and their percentage shares in total population are: members emphasising the spiritual mission of the Church (29%), members emphasising Church rites (28%), members emphasising the Church's aid function (27%) and those as members with loose justification (16%). i.e. members who have no particular reason for their own membership.

34   Niemelä 2006a, 195.

Although young adults do not typically think that in actions note should be taken of history and tradition, there is at least one point at which traditions have an effect: rites of passage. Young adults frequently want ceremonies connected to rites of passage for themselves. Despite a decline in the popularity of getting married in church among others, nine out of ten of the young adults interviewed would, in the event of their possibly getting married, want to do so in church. Getting married in church was justified above all by reasons of tradition. Reasons connected with tradition include among others a church wedding as part of a splendid family party and the church as a fine setting for a wedding. There seemed to be a connection between a church wedding and a big party. Many did not appear to know that it is possible to be married in church even without a big wedding celebration.[35]

A critical attitude to institutions can also be seen in the young adults' somewhat low confidence in the Church and other institutions. Not only the Church, but also other traditional institutions, such as the political parties and the trade union movement do not enjoy much trust among young people. According to the Youth Barometer survey 2006 of Finns aged 15–29, those with a lot of confidence in the Church amounted to 15 per cent, with a further 39 per cent reporting confidence to some extent. Every fifth (18%) reported no confidence in the Church. The share of young people with at least some confidence in the Church has fallen 14 percentage points in ten years between 1996 and 2006 (from 68% to 54%) (See Figure 10).[36]

Those far from the Church especially consider that the Church as a regulatory institution has fallen behind the times, and that there is no room for different kinds of people and a wide diversity of views. Those far from the Church felt that the Church was an environment which did little to support their endeavours at spiritual growth. Many young adults also had experiences or feelings that they were "not good enough" people for Church circles; they felt that their understanding of religion or the way they thought of life did not "fulfil" Church's criteria. Those whose

---

35   Siltala 2006, 151–153; 2005, 50–52.
36   Uskon asia 2006, 48–50.

drifting away from the Church was most advanced had either begun to "suss out" different alternatives and communities in which it was "spiritually easier to breathe", or then they had totally dropped out of organised religion. The relationship to the Church is indicative of lack of confidence. No confidence developed because people felt that they were unable to be themselves.

Figure 10. Confidence in institutions among Finns aged 15–29 (Youth Barometer 1996 and 2006.) %.[37]

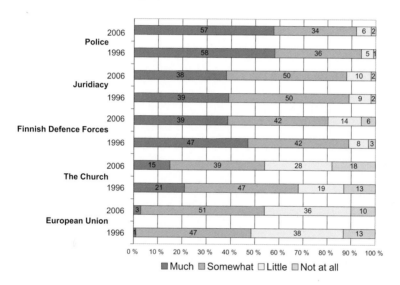

Is the Church anything for me?

The new law on religious freedom was approved in Finland in 2003.[38] After that the number those leaving the Church have

---

37   Uskon asia 2006.

38   In 1923 a law on freedom of religion was passed in Finland according to which new religions could be freely founded and people might freely move from one religion to another. The Constitution guaranteed freedom of religion. State and Church, however, did not entirely part company. In practice, over the years, State and Church have gradually drifted apart. However, many characteristics originating in the union of State and Church persist in society. The opening of

been higher than ever before (see Figure 11). In 2005 and 2006 those leaving the Church amounted to 0.8 per cent of hurch members. Most of those leaving the Church are indeed young adults. About three out of four of those leaving the Church are 18–39-year-old young adults. The numbers of those leaving the Church are especially high among those aged 18–29. Very often the person resigning from the Church is a young adult from the metropolitan area, i.e. just the type of person who is the subject of the present study. In the parish of Kallio there have been relatively more resignations than elsewhere in Finland in the parishes of the Evangelical Lutheran Church.

Figure 11. Those leaving the Church and those received into the Church 1923–2006.

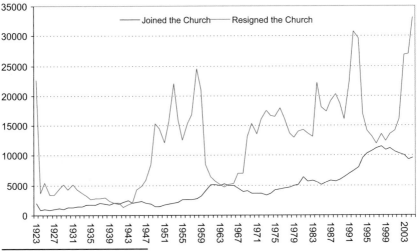

Parliament is marked every year by a church service. The parishes are entitled to levy taxes on their members and are entitled to receive a certain amount from the municipal taxes. The Finnish Defence Forces have in their employ Evangelical Lutheran and Orthodox clergy as military chaplains. The churches are also entitled to solemnize marriages. In schools children and young people receive religious instruction in the Evangelical Lutheran faith or in their own respective religions. Those who do not belong to any religious denomination are offered teaching in civics. Contemplated on the basis of the former development it seems likely that State and Church in Finland will continue to drift further apart. This is not only an outcome of advancing differentiation of religion, but also of the increase in the number of foreigners in the country and the different religious influences they bring with them. EU membership means that Finland belongs to a union in which numerous religions are represented.

Under the new legislation leaving the church became easier. It no longer required a personal visit in order to complete the resignation form. Notice of resignation can also be sent by post to the parish of which the individual was a member or to any registry office. The resignation can be expressed in an individual's own words and no special form is required. Nor is there any longer a month's time for reflection. The resignation is valid as soon as the written notification has been submitted or arrived at the registry office or the parish office of the parish of which the individual concerned is a member. As resignation from the Church became easier under the new legislation there was a further increase in the numbers of young adults resigning.

The option exists to tender one's resignation from the Church to the administrative court by e-mail, and most of those resigning have availed themselves of this easiest way. Of those resigning from the Church in 2006 more than four out if five tendered their resignation by e-mail letter via the net pages of the *Vapaa-ajattelijoiden seura* (the association of free thinkers). Young people especially preferred to use an e-mail letter. This goes to show the great significance of information technology in young adults' lives. The revolution in information technology has also led us to technologically stimulated living and operating environments which create spaces for feelings and actions which are far from the "old reality", i.e. a virtual world typified best by the Internet. In this virtual, and in a sense imaginary world created by the computer large numbers of people are seeking spouses on various dating pages.[39] Indeed, the virtual world has become something of a stepping stone to a traditional, family-like institution. These pages are conducive to the acquisition of a commercial attitude when the objective is to "market oneself" to potential partners by standing out from the crowd. Erich Fromm described taking an attitude at the end of the 1940s, long before the advent of the Internet. According to Fromm a commercial attitude was characteristic of that time. For Fromm this commercial attitude was a person who perceived him/herself as a commodity with an exchange value. A commercially oriented individual saw

---

39   Taira & Väliaho 2006.

his/her own abilities as commodities, whose value was determined according to how well they could be sold on the markets. The self-esteem and dignity of the individual was thus at the mercy of others. The identity of a commercially oriented individual was thus a result of the sum of market roles. Since this individual's objective was to market him/herself, the message to the environment was "*I am the sort that you want.*" The attitudes taken were evasive of more profound emotional ties. Relationships to other people were temporary and superficial and the only permanent characteristic of the orientation was its changeability.[40] Such an attitude challenges the conception of the coherence of an individual's identity if the individual is living simultaneously in the real world and in the illusory dream world created by the media. Even if the virtual world does not break up the individual into various real and imaginary worlds and identities, the Internet has certainly brought about a profound change in our ways of interacting.

However, the reason for the exodus of young people from the Church can hardly be the opportunities of doing so presented by information technology or the easiness of resigning. The reasons lie deeper. Historically, the increase in resignations from the Church occurring in 2003 is not a special phenomenon. Earlier the annual differences in resignations from the Church were not a steady movement; as a consequence of various changes occurring in society and in the Church the numbers have varied greatly (see Figure 11). The research on resignation from the Church shows that there have always been different factors with bearing on resignation. Among others, it was financial problems in the recession years in the early 1990's and a desire to save on Church taxes, in the 1950s it was critical attitudes to the Church after the wars and in the 1970s it was the critical attitude taken to religion in the spirit of the New Left. Nowadays what lies behind resignation from the Church is often the feeling that church and faith no longer have any personal relevance. This is particularly marked in young adults. Many resignations from the Church also constitute a protest and a stance against the decision-making and directions taken by the Church – in practice frequently against the lines taken by

---

40   Fromm 1965, 82–98, 130–131. Cf. Riesman 1953, v–vi.

individual Church employees. The resignation of old people is frequently attributable to disapp ointments in personally significant situations. About 10 per cent of all those leaving the Church join another religious organisation.[41]

As a young adult, a person is strongly focused on him/herself, as has been noted earlier. Personal significance is also greatly sought through Church membership. A total of 124 of those 1,000 interviewed in the Helsinki metropolitan area had resigned from the Church at some point in their lives. The reason for so doing was generally the feeling that the Church held no personal meaning for them. For 90 per cent of them the lack of subjective significance of the Church was at least somewhat behind the reasons for leaving the Church (see Figure 12). The fact that the Church had no personal meaning was an important or very important reason for almost two out of three.

Figure 12. Reasons for leaving the Church among young adults (20–39 years) living in the Helsinki metropolitan area. (Telephone Survey Young Adults in the Helsinki Metropolitan Area 2004, N=124.) %.

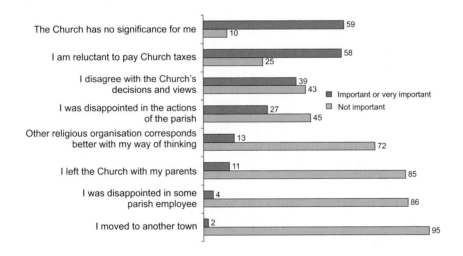

---

41   See Niemelä 2006a; [in press].

The young adults considered it almost equally important that they did not want to pay Church taxes. For only one in four was this of no significance at all. However, reluctance to pay was closely connected to the fact that they felt the Church was of no personal significance. In practice there were only few in the data for whom reluctance to pay Church taxes was not connected to perceiving no personal meaning in the Church.

Considering the Church to be of no personal importance is generally associated with not believing in the teachings of the Church. Those who have resigned from the Church are typically far from the Church teachings. Only 12 per cent of young adults in the metropolitan region and 7 per cent of young Kallio adults who had resigned from the Church firmly believed that Jesus is the Son of God. The majority of those who had resigned from the Church do not believe at all (in the metropolitan area 60% and in Kallio 71%). When a young adult does not believe in the Church teaching, membership of the Church is seen to be at odds with the individual's own thinking, and leaving the Church is justified often by honesty: because one cannot make a commitment to the message of the Church membership is seen as insincerity towards oneself and others.[42] Belonging to the Church merely for the sake of tradition is thus not enough. As noted earlier, the fact that the Church is part of being Finnish is not sufficient reason for young adults.

Finnish religiosity has often been described as "belonging without believing" in contrast to the description of the English as "believing without belonging".[43] However, more and more young adults are challenging this way of thinking. Merely following custom and tradition are not sufficient reasons for belonging to the Church.

Withdrawal often requires an external impulse such as irritation about a position the Church has taken. Young adults typically experience the Church to be too intolerant and conservative. Difference of opinion with the Church's views of decisions had been decisive or almost decisive for 39 per cent of young adults.

42   See Niemelä 2006a, 42–43.
43   See Davie 1994; 2000.

For about equally as many it had no significance. Therefore young adults also quite frequently sense a conflict with some view or decision of the Church. Such a difference of views has frequently set in motion the resignation from the Church of a young person otherwise remote from it. Disappointments with the intolerance of the Church and inequality are very typical for young adults. These disappointments were most often related to the Church' views on homosexuality and female ministry.[44] Young adults in the Church are particularly offended by the poor realisation of human rights. In the eyes of young adults the Church appears judgemental and narrow-minded, and particularly in the case of *"matters of tolerance, whatever they might be, does one live together in marriage or not and does one live with a man or a woman"*. Such things are deemed the individual's own choice, which others, including the Church, should respect. However, they are *"such personal matters that the Church should no longer be putting its nose in"*. The interviewees felt that in its thoughts, values and actions the Church was not living in the modern world with regard to these matters. The way in which the Church had drifted apart from the modern world and the way in which young people were drifting away from the Church culminated to a great extent in the question whether homosexuals and lesbians were entitled to live as they wanted. This and the issue of the ordaining of women as priests largely determined one's attitude to the Church. In the opinion of many the Church's conception of the pair relationship as a whole was old-fashioned and too stiff. Also, in the opinion of the religiously active minority, the Church is not sufficiently bold in taking a stand.[45] Young adults themselves generally accept different kinds of pair relationships. According to the Youth Barometer survey of 2006 homosexual relationships were accepted by 57 per cent of young Finns aged 15-29. Even more (69%) accepted the registration of same-sex unions.[46] The attitudes of the Church to moral questions may even activate those active in the Church to drift away from it. Some of those

44　See Niemelä 2006a, 111–129.
45　Siltala 2005, 93, 96.
46　Uskon asia 2006, 30.

interviewed who had been actively involved in the work of the parish commented that the unbending views of the Church were factors which had caused them to feel that the Church was remote.[47] It is no wonder if the feeling is that *"the Church is nothing for me"* if it is felt to be so remote from one's own thinking. Young adults in the metropolitan area, like their peers elsewhere in Finland, differ from other Finns through a more tenuous bond with the Church and its values.

For only one young adult in four who had left the Church was there anything slight in the background regarding some other religious organisation being more appropriate for the individual concerned (see Figure 12). For every seventh this had been an important reason. One in ten reported that what was decisive was the solution of their own parents or leaving the Church together with their own parents. Personal disappointments with church employees were very seldom the reason for young adults leaving the Church. Moving to live in another place underlay leaving the Church for only very few young adults interviewed. However, practical experience has shown that a change in the life situation and place of residence, such as moving to the place of study and beginning an independent life tend to trigger resignation. Yet there are actually other underlying reasons for resignation than the move itself, such as perceiving the Church as an institution without personal meaning.

Breaking away from Church teaching

One out of ten (11%) of the young adults living in the metropolitan area and 7 per cent of those living in Kallio considered faith/religion very important (see Figure 13). A further 15 per cent considered it fairly important (13% in Kallio). For every fifth in Helsinkin metropolitan area and more than one third (37%) in Kallio religion was of no importance whatsoever. Religion was more important for women and men, likewise for

---

47   Siltala 2006, 161.

those over 30 it was more important than for those under 30 (see Appendix 1). Almost half of the young Kallio men (43%) considered religion a totally unimportant matter in their lives (likewise 30% of women). Moreover, the longer an individual has lived in the metropolitan area the more indifferent to religion s/he is.

Figure 13. Importance of faith/religion among young adults aged 20–39 living in the metropolitan area and in Kallio. (Telephone Survey Young Adults in Kallio 2004, N=500; Telephone Survey Young Adults in the Helsinki Metropolitan Area 2004, N=1,000.) %.

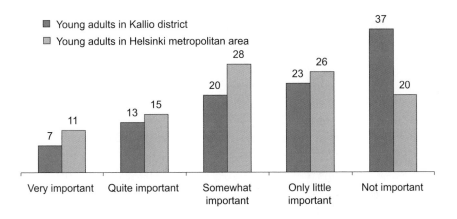

Compared to the rest of Finland, young adults in both Kallio and the entire metropolitan area are somewhat more indifferent in their relationship to religion. According to the *World Values 2005* survey one out of three Finns aged 20–39 considered faith/religion fairly important or very important.[48] The corresponding figure for all Finns was almost one half (45%).

The share of those distant from the Church among the young adults living in Kallio is especially large. Figure 14 illustrated the difference between all Finns, young adults in the Helsinki

---

48   Of all Finns aged 20–39 13% considered religion as very important and 21% fairly important (World Values 2005).

metropolitan area, in Kallio and in the rest of Finland. The figure shows the shares in these population groups of those believing that Jesus is the Son of God. Only one out of four of the young Kallio adults reported believing or deeming it probable that Jesus is the Son of God. Of young adults living elsewhere in the metropolitan area almost half think in this way and elsewhere in Finland two out of three. The share of all Finns believing firmly that Jesus is the Son of God or at least thinking this likely is more than two thirds.[49]

Figure 14. Belief of all Finns and young adults in Jesus as the Son of God. (Gallup Ecclesiastica 2003, N=1009; Telephone Survey Young Adults in Kallio 2004, N=500; Telephone Survey Young Adults in the Helsinki Metropolitan Area 2004, N=1,000.) %.

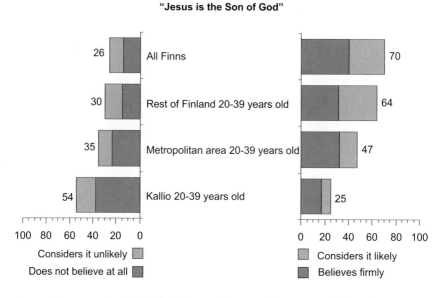

According to the World Values Survey four out of five (74%) of all Finns say that they believe in some way in the existence of God. Half of Finns (49%) believe in *one* God. Several studies clearly show that fewer than one in ten Finns declares that they do not believe in the existence of God at all. Belief in God was weaker among young adults in the metropolitan area (50%) and

---

49   See Kääriäinen & Niemelä & Ketola 2005, 106.

notably weaker in Kallio (33%). Among the young adults of Kallio only one out of five reported believing firmly in the existence of God, and among the young adults of the metropolitan area one out of four (see Table 3). In addition 13 per cent of those in Kallio and 22 per cent in the metropolitan area considered it likely that God existed. In Kallio over one quarter (29%) of young adults did not believe in the existence of God at all, in the whole metropolitan area every sixth (17%). The more specific the Christian faith in question the fewer there are who believe in it (see Table 3). Less than one quarter (23%) of young adults in the metropolitan region and 14 per cent in Kallio believe firmly in God as the Creator of the Earth. Less than one fifth of young adults in the metropolitan area believe that Jesus was born of a Virgin or in the existence of the Devil or Hell. These questions were not in the survey data of the young adults in Kallio.

Table 3. Belief of 20–39 year-olds in the Helsinki metropolitan area (and in brackets in Kallio) in certain Christian tenets. (Telephone Survey Young Adults in the Helsinki Metropolitan Area 2004, N=1,000; Telephone Survey Young in Kallio, N=500.) %.

	Believes firmly	Considers it likely	In the middle	Considers it unlikely	Does not believe at all
God exists	28 (20)	22 (13)	20 (20)	13 (18)	17 (29)
God has created the World	23 (14)	13 (6)	19 (16)	15 (16)	30 (48)
Jesus is the Son of God	32 (17)	15 (8)	18 (20)	12 (16)	23 (38)
Jesus was born of a Virgin	20	11	18	14	36
Jesus' teachings and precepts for life are valid in our time	26	32	25	12	6
The Devil exists	19	10	18	18	35
Angels exist	24	19	19	13	26
Heaven exists	27	19	20	12	22
Hell exists	17	10	23	16	34

The Italian philosopher *Gianni Vattimo* in his work *I believe that I believe* writes that it is obvious that the average modern person does not accept Christianity or choose belief on the moral level. In his opinion the same goes for the level of doctrinal structures. Acceptance does not occur because the many moral tenets and doctrinal structures of Christianity appear "scandalous" to the modern person. According to Vattimo the text of the Gospel seems to need a liberal dose of myth-breaking in order to appeal to the modern person with an average level of cultivation.[50] In the minds of those remote from the Church and those young adults considering resignation from the Church, the Church was not only far from itself in values and spiritually, but also intellectually retarded. This view was due in part to experiences of religious education in childhood and youth. These young adults felt that they had grown out of the religiosity they were taught as children. Their childhood faith had not matured as they grew older. The Church's way of conveying its message might originally even have been felt to be intellectually blasphemous. One interviewee reported feeling even as a child that it was *"terrible offensive"* that Bible stories were taught as facts, from which there came *"a certain feeling of illogicality and of confusion that things like that cannot be true"*. The interviewee stated that since religious instruction in childhood had gone onto such a *"low and demeaning level"*, later it was *"terribly difficult to take religion seriously in any way at all"*. As the interviewee grew up it was necessary for her to find "my very own way of processing religiosity".

According to this interviewee the Church has *"lost the game as far as adults are concerned"*, because the fact that at the very beginning the teaching of religion was *"telling fairytales"*, this deprived other possibly good ways of teaching religion of their credibility. The interviewee was disturbed by the fact that the conveying of the message has got stuck on the Sunday school level and literal interpretation of the Bible.

The telephone interview data as a whole shows that Christian doctrines do not in general have much impact on young adults. Those young people especially who are considering resigning from the Church are extremely dubious about Christian beliefs. Of the young people considering leaving the Church only one in ten believed that God created the world. Over one third of those who could not imagine themselves leaving the Church believed firmly in God as the Creator of the World. As noted earlier, the young

---

50   Vattimo 1999, 60.

adults in Kallio were consistently more sceptical towards Christian beliefs.

Table 4. Belief of young adults in the metropolitan area (in Kallio in parentheses) in various Christian doctrines (percentage of those firmly believing) on the basis of commitment to the Church. (Telephone Survey Young Adults in the Helsinki Metropolitan Area 2004, N=1,000; Telephone Survey Young in Kallio, N=500.) %.

		Believes firmly that God has created the world	Believes firmly that Jesus is the Son of God
Church members	Could not imagine leaving the Church	42 (35)	54 (34)
	Has not considered leaving	24 (19)	37 (24)
	Has considered leaving but did not	11 (9)	18 (21)
	May leave	8 (11)	16 (10)
Non Church members	Has considered joining	34 (12)	36 (18)
	Has not considered joining	27 (7)	31 (5)
	Could not imagine joining	19 (4)	21 (7)
All		23 (14)	32 (17)

In the Kallio district there are very few young adults who belong to the Evangelical Lutheran Church of Finland and who on the basis of the interview data could be called "firmly committed to Christianity". Examination of the telephone data in order to select such individuals for personal interview proved unexpectedly laborious. After a lengthy process 12 young adults were found from the telephone data on 500 who both consented to be interviewed face-to-face and fulfilled the criteria "Church members strongly committed to Christianity.[51] This small minority

---

51 According to the telephone interviews the individuals selected for interview face-to-face had the following in common: they had completed confirmation classes, they were members of the Evangelical Lutheran Church of Finland, and considered religion an extremely important matter for them. They also firmly believed in the following tenets of Christianity "There is some higher power", "God exists", "God created the world", and "Jesus is the Son of God". They moreover attended divine service at least a few times a year. On the basis of this initial information it was assumed that the interviewees were committed

strongly committed to Christianity alone showed that they are an internally varied group in whose lives faith and the Church are apparent in many ways. Some went with the Church mainstream and in many ways were representative of members of the traditional church of the people. For them faith was a markedly private matter and in spite of their commitment to the Church and to Christianity they were passive in their religious observances. Some on the other hand represented the revivalist view of faith, when faith has a strong and holistic role in the young adult's life. They had often arrived at some religious resolution of their own or at some point in their lives had an experience which served to strengthen their faith. They frequently criticised the Church strongly for its lack of backbone and for not being faithful enough to the Bible. For this reason they did not generally participate in the activities of the Church, but were active in the revivalist activities of some church. For the third group of young adults committed to the Church, faith had a marked societal component. They wanted more transparency in the Church and self-criticism. These young people were especially disappointed because they felt that equality does not operate within the Church and that, for example, the Church discriminated against homosexuals and women as priests. Since they are frequently disappointed in the line taken by the Church they are not generally willing to participate in its activities.[52] This different attitude among young adults firmly committed to Christianity reflects the same division into religiously liberal and religiously conservative which divides the entire Christian field and also religious organisations throughout the world.[53]

---

to Christianity and on this basis they were interviewed in greater depth for their thoughts on Christianity and their own religiosity by means of semi-structured theme interviews. Hyvönen 2006, 85–86.

52   Hyvönen 2006, 89–102.

53   In the field of religion these tendencies represent two utterly different ways of perceiving the religious challenges occasioned by modernisation, diversification of values and change in lifestyles. See Wuthnow 1988; 1989; Beyer 1994.

Diversification in religious values

Over the years belief "in some form" of God has not declined in the population as a whole, nor have there been changes in the importance of God. However, firm attachment to Christian beliefs has clearly declined. This indicates the subjectification of religious belief and shows that it has become of the *à la carte* type.

The attitudes of young adults to religious tradition and religious beliefs are typically relative and pluralistic. The content of beliefs is for them clearly not the core content of religion; instead the emphasis is on human ethics in a general sense. A clear majority of the young adults did not believe that any single religion is the only real truth. Only 14 per cent of the young adults in the metropolitan area totally or partially agreed with the statement "there is only one true religion" (see Table 5). Respondents totally or partially disagreeing with the statement totalled three quarters. Thus a large number of those who believe in God and consider themselves religious do not perceive their religiosity in an exclusive light. The longer a young adult has lived in the metropolitan area the more s/he was likely to disagree with the statement "there is only one true religion" (p=.002).

Of the young adults in the metropolitan area those considering leaving the Church most frequently denied that there was only one true religion (see Figure 15). Likewise those who could not imagine themselves joining the Church typically denied the existence of one true religion. In the personal interviews those considering resignation from the Church often reported that there were many level and types of religiosity and it was thought that in many different religions there is an articulation of some world morality whose basic tenets can be found, for example, in the UN Declaration of Human Rights. Adherence to this was considered to emanate from the individual him/herself, not from the will of some external power. What was called for from the Church was an ethical and moral institution to bring humanity and humane values to the fore in modern times.

Figure 15. Proportion of young adults in the Helsinki metropolitan area, who totally disagree with statement "There is only one true religion" (Telephone Survey Young Adults in the Helsinki Metropolitan Area 2004, N=1,000.) %.

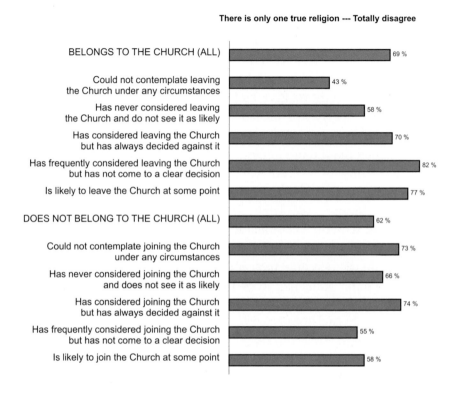

A quarter (29%) of the young adults in the metropolitan region was interested in taking on board influences from different religions. Equally many were interested in matters pertaining to spirituality and happy to seek for new elements for their world views. The young adults particularly keen to take on board influences from other religions are those on the edge of Church membership, i.e. those either considering resignation from the Church or those considering joining it. They are also the most interested in alternative religious movements and world views. All in all one quarter (24%) was interested in buying literature on spirituality.

Table 5. Conceptions of the relativity of religion and interest in spiritual and world view questions among young adults aged 20-39 in the metropolitan area. (Telephone Survey Young Adults in the Helsinki Metropolitan Area 2004, N=1,000.) %.

	Totally agree	Partly agree	Neither agree or disagree	Partly disagree	Totally disagree	Total
There is only one true religion	9	5	10	13	63	100
I like to take on board influences from different religions	9	20	23	22	27	100
I am interested in spiritual matters and like to look for new elements for my world view	9	22	22	28	19	100
I could buy spiritual literature	9	16	14	25	37	100
I am interested in alternative religious movements and world views	3	9	11	27	50	100

These figures reveal an openminded and relative attitude to religion. No religion is considered to represent the only real truth, but many feel that in religions there is something from which they think they can absorb influences. Thus it can be claimed that attitudes to religions are positive, but relative and critical. They are thought to contain something valuable, although none of them alone represents the whole truth. Thus distance is clearly being taken from religious authorities.[54]

Although attitudes to Christian beliefs are selective and sceptical, as many as 58 per cent of young adults in the metropolitan area consider it at least likely that the teachings of Jesus are appropriate as a guideline in life for our own times. In other words, many more believe in Jesus' guidelines for living than believe in His divinity or in the Virgin birth. This finding shows that what is positive and worth learning in religions is their pan-human ethical teaching. This religious emphasis on pan-human ethics is characteristic of those of liberal religious tendencies in the USA and Northern Europe.[55]

54 Ketola 2006, 308–309.
55 Ketola 2006, 309.

Among those questioning membership the ethics seeking to promote human rights, solidarity between people and environmental protection flourished. Indeed, it can be stated that the main religious attitude of Christianity, love,[56] was vital for them. Those who were still members of the Church but considering resignation actually justified their membership of the Church or the passing on of religious tradition from generation to generation by the fact that they concur in this value base of the Church and by being members wished to help their less fortunate neighbours even though membership of the Church did not give them anything. By being members they gave something to someone else.

Alternative channels for spiritual search

Where is the spiritual searching of young adults channelled if not through the traditional religious beliefs and institutions? The findings show that there is very little support for folk beliefs such as witchcraft, ghosts or astrology in Kallio and elsewhere in the metropolitan area – much less than there is support for Christian beliefs. However, it is worth noting that in contrast to Christian beliefs, young adults in the metropolitan area and especially in Kallio believe in certain folk beliefs slightly more often than do other Finns. Young adults in Kallio and throughout the metropolitan area believed more generally than other Finns above all in the existence of unidentified flying objects (UFOs) and ghosts, and that it is possible to influence another person's life through witchcraft. All in all just over one tenth of the young adults believed firmly or to some extent in ghosts and witchcraft. As many as one quarter of young Kallio adults and one fifth of young adults in the metropolitan area believe to some extent in UFOs. The young adults in the metropolitan area and in Kallio believe as little or even less than do the rest of Finns in the powers of mediums to transmit messages from the deceased or in astrology or in telling the future with playing cards. However, those firmly believing in these amount to less than two percent.

---

56   Smart 2005, 31.

Of the beliefs elicited, belief in UFOs was the only one in which more young men than young women believed. Every fourth young man in the metropolitan area considered that the existence of UFOs was at least probable, the corresponding figure for women was 13 per cent.[57]

Figure 16. Folk beliefs. (Telephone Survey Young Adults in the Helsinki Metropolitan Area 2004, N=1,000, in which young adults living in Kallio N=55; and Church Monitor 2004, N=2.569). %.

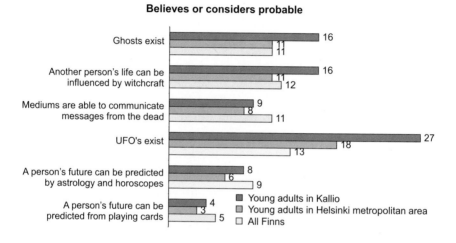

Believes or considers probable

This raises the question of the men's longing for the mysterious projected onto Space. Exciting stories in the movies and television are frequently set in Space – in a global world there are no longer

---

57   The UFO cult is a system of beliefs revolving around Unidentified Flying Objects. From the perspective of examining world views UFO cults are particularly interesting as they combine religiosity and science and a questioning of the human and earth-centred world view. UFO cults include the notion that there is intelligent life on other planets than Earth and that it is possible to make contact with this life. The individual's world view has been challenged by experiences in which representatives of life which have come from elsewhere (frequently referred to as humanoids) or their vehicles (i.e. UFOs) have been encountered. See Saliba 1995, 48–51. The consequences with regard to world view and ethics are notably of experiences of abduction in which humanoids have carried people off. See Whitmore 1995, 75. Those who have experienced an abduction phenomenon consider that what is in the background is frequently the promotion of an individual's spiritual development or the conveying of an ecological message to humanity.

remote corners except in Space. Space allows the mysterious and the imagination free rein.

It may also be that the mysterious dimension is pursued through the mass media. Among others, men who had left the Church sought a mysterious dimension in life through legends and stories like The Lord of the Ring. In the lives of men who had left the Church the stories were mostly connected with films and alongside these, literature. Through these the interviewees mirrored themselves and their relation to other people, to the world and to the supernatural. The interviewees were particularly interested in various growth and survival stories. They considered it important that one should be able to identify with the characters in the films and seek interface from one's own experiences. One man reported processing questions relating to his father's death with the help of films. In the best cases the story in the film or book dovetailed in with the individual's personal story. Experiencing the mysterious might also manifest itself in the form of fantasy. One of the interviewees was emphatic in stressing the need for another reality, which in this case was the world of fantasy books and role play. This interviewee had been fascinated by fantasy stories ever since childhood, and described the fantasy world as a kind of substitute for religion. Fantasy was the opposite of the routine world of physics; the most important thing was to be able to imagine and believe. The criteria of the scientific world did not extend into the fantasy reality. There were also elements of communality in the development of the fantasy world into a cult. Role-plays were played together and friends discussed the books together. The interviewee also said that in the future he wanted to pass on the stories of the fantasy world to his children.[58]

A perfectly good church nevertheless

On a general level the attitudes of young adults to the Church are not negative. Of the young people in the metropolitan area belonging to the Church only one per cent have a decidedly

---

58   Kosunen 2006, 263–277.

negative attitude to the Church and seven percent a somewhat negative attitude (see Figure 17). More than half the young adults are positively disposed towards the Church. Every third image of the Church is neutral. Most of those who have resigned from the Church have a positive or neutral image of it. Only six percent of those who have left the Church have an extremely negative attitude towards it, with 24 per cent somewhat negatively disposed.

Figure 17. Image of the Church among those in the metropolitan area aged 20–39 years who have resigned and those who belong to the Church. (Telephone Survey Young Adults in the Helsinki Metropolitan Area 2004, N=1,000.) %.

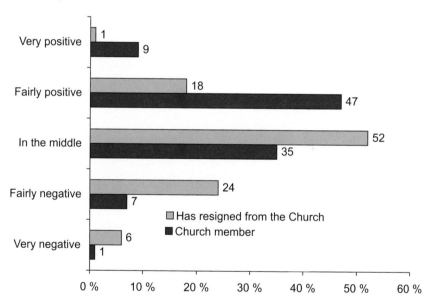

Comparison of the image of the Church among Finns of different ages reveals a great difference between young and old Finns regarding the extent to which the Church is perceived to be needed (F=13.22***): typically young people do not personally perceive the Church as a necessary institution. Of Finns aged less than 30 only 12 per cent reported that there is a clear need for the Church (chose number 5 on a scale 1-5), while the corresponding figure for those over 70 years old was 58 per cent. However, there was no difference in the estimates of respondents of different ages as to whether the Church is perceived to be service-minded, the defender of the weak or unselfish.[59]

In spite of a non-existent or tenuous connection to the parish of Kallio, the young people who were far from the Church did not typically have a negative impression of the parish of Kallio even though these young people felt and perceived activities through what they did not want them to be – divine service and *"tea-drinking among the religious"* where Jesus is shoved in as an extra, likewise a view of what is the right and wrong way to live. Contemplating the Church institution on a general level the interviewee had an impression of a distant and unwelcoming church.

> *...if I were to go, let's say, next Friday to one of those parish tea sessions, well, I think that I would not be welcomed with open arms in the way they say, that "come on here, everybody has a good time and the guitar is playing". But I would argue that the guitar would stop playing and everybody would turn round and gape, who's that, and it would take a minute before they say anything.*

On the other hand, not only as a residential area, but also as a parish, Kallio was found by many to be diverse and tolerant in contrast to the way the Evangelical Lutheran Church was seen in general. Young adults considering resignation from the Church among others described their impression of the parish of Kallio and the Kallio Church as being *"extremely positive"* and *"close to the people"*. Kallio church was seen to be a church which *"appears to be a church for the people and not a church for the Church"*. It as also felt that Kallio Church arranged *"the greatest courses which are somehow really close to the people of today, all sorts of painting and retreats and who knows what"*, *" where anybody at all could certainly go and not need to be a great Holy Joe to dare to join in"*.

The parish of Kallio has indeed been very innovative in its activities. The new types of activity have proved successful. Ever

---

59   See Niemelä 2006b, 60.

since 1995 the parish of Kallio has arranged short courses for adults of working age in creative expression, and these have become extremely popular. They include courses in painting lasting a few days and various other courses in creative expression where a person can use painting, movement, music or writing as a means of self-expression. There is a fee for these courses. The courses started off because of concern in the parish in the early 1990s regarding the future of parish group meetings which had been operation for years but which were now attracting new participants. The number of participants in Bible and prayer circles had dropped by half in five years in the 1990s. On the other hand changing the focus of activities to short courses there was a manifold increase in participation within a short space of time. In 2004 participants in courses arranged by the parish of Kallio amounted to almost 1,000, with 100 participating in retreats. The short courses of the parish of Kallio have become the most popular form of activity with adults. The activities with adults of the parish of Kallio are overall one sixth of the work with adults of all the Helsinki parishes, even though the population of Kallio is only 6 per cent of the population of all the Helsinki parishes combined. These courses attract above all women of working age across parish borders from all over the metropolitan area. The interviews with participants show that many of them were not involved in other parish activity. Many people felt it was easier to commit to a course lasting a few days than to the traditional form in the parish of a group for a whole longer term.[60]

Young adults in the activities of the Church

Although almost two out of three Finns consider themselves religious, public religious practice is at a low level in all age groups in Finland. Accorging to World Value Survey 2005 one out of six (14%) attend some religious activity at least once a month. Almost half (45%) of Finns attend religious activities less often than once a month, but at least once a year. One in five attend

60   Harvola 2006, 134–147.

religious functions less often than once a year, and one in four (26%) practically never attend. In European comparison Finland is placed at the tail-end and approximately on the same level as neighbouring areas – the other Nordic countries, Russia and the Baltic States. Church attendance has been decreasing in the 20th and 21st century, ever since there has been reliable information available for comparison on the subject. The decline can also be seen in other traditional regularly arranged events.

Young adults are even more passive than the average Finns. More than half attend religious services or other occasions less than once a year or then not at all. Of the young adults in the metropolitan area only about 7 per cent attend religious services at least once a month. About the same amount (8%) – and the same individuals – attend other religious occasions at least once month. The young adults of the metropolitan area do not differ from their peers elsewhere in Finland in their religious observances. Elsewhere in Finland, too, young adults are equally passive and also more passive than the older age groups. Young adults resident in the Kallio district are even more passive than their peers when it comes to attending religious occasions; only four per cent attend divine service or other occasion at least once a month, and almost two thirds attend less than once a year.

Like those reporting that they consider religion important, those who are religiously active are often people who have moved to the metropolitan area from elsewhere and who have lived there for a short time. They are more often women than men and are generally over 30 years old.

In the private practice of religion, too, young adults are more passive than older people, and the young adults of Kallio are even more passive. Every sixth (16%) young adult in the metropolitan area prays every day (Kallio 12%), every third (33%) does not pray at all (Kallio 41%). In reading the Bible, too, the young adults of Kallio are more passive than other young adults (see Table 7).[61] Religious radio programmes and religious music are listened to

---

61 Every tenth (9%) Kallio resident aged 20–39 reads the Bible once a month. Among all those in the metropolitan area the share is 12% and among young adults living elsewhere 13%. Of all Finns every fifth (18%) reads the Bible at least once a month.

only seldom, and in Kallio even less than among other young adults. However, most of the young adults do read the free parish magazine distributed to the home of all Church members. Only every third young adult reported never reading these (of those belonging to the Church, every fourth).

All in all, Finnish religiosity is by nature private. Although Finns are not very regular in attending public religious activities, nevertheless religion is a prominent part of many people's lives. Although in public religious practice Finland is placed at the tail-end of Europe, it is placed in well above the European average in terms of how many Finns pray. Only one in five Finns say that they never pray, while one in three of all Europeans say so. A quarter of Finns pray daily, and sixteen per cent at least once a week. Half of all Finns, as of all Europeans, pray at least once a month. The religiosity of young adults is also decidedly private. Most of the young people reporting that they consider religion important and praying regularly are passive in the public observation of religion. Young people do not perceive religious institutions to be as important of themselves as do the older generations, as has already been noted.

Table 6. Participation of young Kallio adults (and in brackets young adults in the Helsinki metropolitan area) in Church services, other religious occasions and Church rites. (Telephone Survey Young Adults in the Helsinki Metropolitan Area 2004, N = 1,000; Telephone Survey Young in Kallio, N=500.) %.

	At least once a month	Several times a year	At least once a year	Less than once a year	Not at all in recent years	Total
Attends services	4 (7)	8 (8)	27 (29)	24 (23)	38 (30)	100 %
Attends other religious occasions	4 (8)	5 (5)	9 (15)	15 (19)	66 (51)	100 %
Has been present at Church rites such as baptisms, weddings, funerals	1 (1)	17 (23)	50 (52)	27 (22)	4 (2)	100 %

87

Table 7. Private practice of religion of young Kallio adults (and in brackets the Helsinki metropolitan area). (Telephone Survey Young Adults in the Helsinki Metropolitan Area 2004, N=1,000; Telephone Survey Young in Kallio, N=500.) %.

	Daily	At least once a week	At least once a month	At least once a year	Less than once a year	Not at all in recent years	Total
Prays	12 (16)	10 (13)	14 (12)	12 (15)	11 (11)	41 (33)	100 %
Reads the Bible	1 (3)	2 (3)	6 (6)	17 (17)	15 (18)	59 (53)	100 %
Reads church magazine or other Christian publications or literature	0 (1)	22 (23)	24 (25)	10 (12)	7 (5)	36 (33)	100 %
Listens to spiritual or religious programs on radio	0 (1)	1 (3)	4 (4)	4 (6)	7 (8)	83 (78)	100 %
Listens to Christian music	1 (3)	4 (5)	8 (10)	10 (14)	11 (10)	65 (58)	100 %

Church rites, however, do indeed reach also the most passively religious young adults (see Table 6). Of young adults in the metropolitan area 74 per cent attend Church rites at least once a year, and only few young adults have not taken part at all in recent years. In the religiously passive area of Kallio, too, the share of those attending once a year is 68 per cent. Of its various modes of action, the Church reaches young adults above all at the performance of Church rites. However, there has been a fall in the popularity of various Church rites, above all in Church weddings, and only 61 per cent of couples were married in church in 2006.[62]

It became clear above that only 4 per cent of the young adults of Kallio and 7-8 per cent of the young adults of the metropolitan area attend church services and other religious occasions at least

---

62 In 2005, out of a total population of 5 million, Church rites were attended by more than 4 million. Church rites moreover reach the majority of those who otherwise seldom go to church. Church rites reach the majority of Finns at various stages of their lives: 84% of newborn children were baptised by the Evangelical Lutheran Church of Finland in 2006, 88% of 15 year-olds went through confirmation classes and confirmation, 61% were married by the Church and about 97% of those who died had a church funeral. The statistics for funerals and confirmation have remained at high level for decades. However, the share of those baptised has fallen slightly (92% in 1980; 86% in 1995 and 84% in 2006). The greatest decrease has been in the number of those married in church: In 2006 the percentage of all those married in church was 61, whereas in 1995 it was 78. However, every tenth marriage in a registry office is given a Church blessing. Kääriäinen & Niemelä & Ketola 2003, 180; Kirkko muutosten keskellä 2004, 122; Kirkon tilastollinen vuosikirja 2005; Church Statistics 2006.

once a month. Might young adults have some potential interest in the activities of the parish? Every third young adult in the metropolitan area – including those belonging to the Church – and almost half of the young Kallio adults report that that whatever and whenever the Church were to arrange something, they would never participate (See Figure 18). A further 12 per cent would attend less than once a year. Nevertheless, there are quite a few young adults who would like to participate more in religious occasions: In the metropolitan are one fifth (21%) and in Kallio (17%) of young adults would be interested to attend religions occasions at least once a month if meaningful opportunities were available and at suitable times. Thus there are in Kallio five times more interested in attending than there are in the active group, and in the metropolitan area three times as many. Many of them are such people who at present hardly ever attend Church activities.

Figure 18. Interest among young adults in Kallio and in the metropolitan area in attending religions occasions and present attendance.[63] (Telephone Survey Young Adults in the Helsinki Metropolitan Area 2004, N=1,000; Telephone Survey Young in Kallio, N=500.) %.

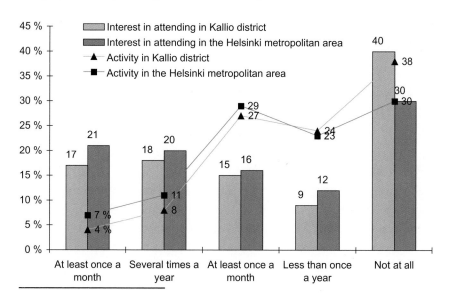

---

63   Present religious participation refers to attendance at divine service. Examination of participation at other occasions would hardly alter the share of active people.

Why then are the activities of the Church not found to be interesting or meaningful? Often young adults have not found that it is something for them and they have felt no need, or have not felt that they are the ones addressed. The message of the Church and the activities of the parish were simply felt to be alien. However, it is not necessarily the case that the young adults felt that they had drifted away from the Church, but rather that the Church had drifted away from them and their everyday lives. The great stumbling block was felt to be the confined nature of spirituality or confession of faith and narrowness.[64]

The nature of the parish, the mission and the modes of work had as a whole remained largely obscure to those considering resignation from the Church and among interviewees who had already left the Church. Those who were far from the Church encountered it by chance at family gatherings involving the Church. Those considering resignation from the Church did not even wish for any religious activity for themselves as over half of them (53%) had no desire to attend religious occasions even if they were arranged according to their own wishes and their own schedules did not prevent participation. Even among those considering joining the Church about one third (31%) were of this opinion.

Expectations of the Church and Church activities

Many young adults required that there should be the right "atmosphere" in participation, that the others present should be "of the same type" and that there should be activity enabling a suitable degree of a feeling "of one's own freedom and a communality that feels good" and in which one might exert influence. Many were of the opinion that this cannot be found with the Church.[65] Those participating in the Church activities also wanted more implementation of the social. Absence of formality

---

64   Wathen 2006, 185.
65   Kumpulainen & Gothoni 2006, 260; see also Wathen 2006, 186–187.

and the opportunity for a certain non-commitment were deemed good. Some were interested in retreats into silence. On the other hand it was felt that it might be easier to participate in large-scale occasions or happenings. The threshold for attending these is lower, as one does not necessarily need to be a very active participant. The participant has the feeling that s/he will be left in peace and that no extensive knowledge will be required. S/he can simply be there.[66] According to *Richard Florida* those belonging to the new creative class make for gatherings characterised by tolerance and transparency and where the threshold is low. According to Florida people in the creative class are extremely selective and avoid places which do not reflect their values or offer them an opportunity to strengthen their own identities. As noted already, many young adults, however, do not feel that the Church reflects their values. The notion of living in a community does indeed appeal to the creative class, but not so much that they would be willing to relinquish their own lives and self-fulfilment. As Florida puts it, what they want is a virtually anonymous community. They prefer loose ties to firm ones.[67]

According to Florida modern communality differs essentially from the old communality. Formerly communities were characterised by close connections and commitment to family, friends and organisations. Now people make for place where they can make friends and meet new people easily and spend a virtually anonymous life. The loosening of ties to people and institutions according to Florida is due to the growth in the number of our ties.[68] Strong ties are generally long-term and they are characterised by trust and reciprocity in many areas of life. Many people have strong ties, like a spouse, close friends and family members. In contrast to what used to be, not even these strong ties, according to Florida, dominate or dictate our lives as much as they used to for many. Loose ties, however, demand less investment and they can be used more opportunistically.

---

66   Wathen 2006, 185–187.
67   Florida 2005, 26, 369, 468.
68   Florida 2005, 49.

What was expected of the parish in addition to loose commitment? Above all, that one could discuss with others various matters pertaining to life, such as human relations, faith, coping, exhaustion and other problems in life. In the eyes of young adults far from the Church, a positive image of the Church came from the concrete aid it dispensed and the support and empathy it offered. As many as one quarter (27%) of the young adults of Kallio had at some time in their lives wanted personal discussion or support involving a member of the clergy. Of those far from the Church or considering resignation one fifth had at some point wanted spiritual support or help, discussion with a member of the clergy or some other Church worker. For those far from the Church it was not a matter of indifference what sort of helper this representative of the parish was. Such a person should be tolerant and understanding. If a young person far from the Church and considering resignation were to turn to a representative of the Church, it was hoped that such a person would have human warmth. It is not required of the Church that it should be "a *moralising institution determining its own opinions*", but rather "*a moral guideline from which it is easy to seek and without feeling any guilt, views and confirmation in times of weakness*". The young adults represented the view according to which in order to be better anchored in the present times the Church should offer more and easier spiritual support. Those far from the Church considered it some kind of an insurance company to which they wished to retain a tie in case other support structures in life should fail them. It was hoped that the Church would be a support structure in life. Even those who were farthest from the Church at times wanted support from it. Support was wanted, among other things, for the everyday routine of the pair relationship. According to the telephone survey 13 per cent of the young adults living in Kallio wanted support from the Church for their pair relationship. Women (15%) wanted such support slightly more than men (10%). Support was wanted most by divorcees, almost half of them, and those living in marriage, of whom one quarter wanted support from the Church. Those wishing support from the Church were in general those who considered religion more important and people who felt positive about their confirmation classes or who had been involved in the youth activities of the parish.[69]

In addition to appreciating the humanitarian and spiritual work of the Church, the interviewees appreciated the involvement of the Church at turning points in one's life, such as baptism, confirmation classes, marriage and burial. Such a turning point might also among other things be starting school. The interviewees also wanted the Church to come among the people, to come where people are, as in workplaces and shopping centres.

Church rites held at turning points in life, such as baptism, marriage and burial provided a natural opportunity for giving support. But do the young adults feel that they get support in such situations? In the telephone interviews conducted with five hundred young adults in the area of the parish of Kallio more than half (61%) reported losing a close person through death in recent years and having attended the funeral in church. These bereaved people were asked if they felt that the actions of the priest conducting the ceremony provided spiritual support. There were considerably fewer people whose marriage had been solemnised or blessed in church or whose own child had been baptised than there were those who had lost someone close to them. They were asked a similar question about these ceremonies (see Table 8). In connection with funerals over half of the respondents felt that the priest had at least to some extent provided spiritual support. Only one out of five reported feeling that the priest provided a great deal of spiritual support. Every fifth also reported that they did not feel the priest provided any spiritual support at all at the funeral. Those whose marriage was solemnised or blessed in church or whose own child had been baptised had felt more positive about the priest for giving spiritual support. Of the young adults as many as 96 per cent felt they had derived at least some spiritual support from the priest, and of those whose marriage was solemnised 85 per cent. Over half felt they had received much or very much of support.[70]

---

69   Siltala 2006, 157; 2005, 31.
70   Laiho 2006, 104–117.

Table 8. Young adults' experiencing the priest as providing spiritual support in connection with Church rites in Kallio. (Telephone Survey Young Adults in Kallio 2004.)

	Baptism (N=23) %	Marriage or blessing of marriage (N=35) %	Burial (N=304) %
Not at all	4	9	21
A little	0	6	21
Some	39	31	36
Much	48	40	16
Very much	9	14	3
Cannot say	0	0	2
Total	100	100	100

Interest in voluntary work

The young adults were particularly positively disposed towards various types of aid work. Many of those interviewed considered the responsibility taken by the Church and its taking care of others to be a good thing overall. The Church was felt to provide some with a meaningful field in which to operate in voluntary work.[71]

The telephone survey also shows that many young people are interested in voluntary work as a whole. Of the thousand young people in the metropolitan interviewed by telephone as many as 29 per cent are involved in some sort of voluntary work, and many others could imagine engaging in this. Only 14 per cent of those not engaged in voluntary work found it impossible to imagine that they would be active in some sector of voluntary work. Thus the attitudes of the young adults on the whole were decidedly positive. The share of those unable to imagine that they would engage in voluntary work was for almost all forms of work elicited clearly less than half of the respondents (see Figure 19). The young people worked most in the sphere of work with children and young people, and it was in this that the greatest interest was also expressed. There was also interest expressed in working with the

---

71   See Wathen 2006.

elderly, the handicapped, in nature conservation and animal welfare and sport.

Figure 19. Activity and interest in various forms of voluntary work among young adults in the metropolitan area. (Telephone Survey Young Adults in the Helsinki Metropolitan Area 2004, N=1,000). %

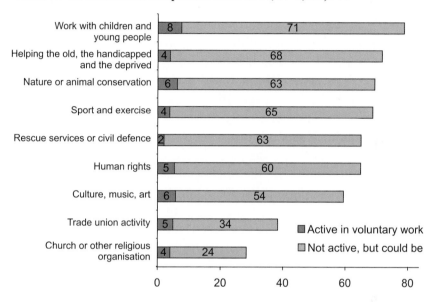

The voluntary work of the Church was reportedly less interesting than any of the other types of voluntary work mentioned. However, in addition to those already engaged in voluntary work for the Church, every fourth young adult in the metropolitan area (24%) and in Kallio every fifth (18%) was potentially interested in voluntary work for the Church. At present only two percent of respondents in Kallio and four percent of respondents in the metropolitan area are engaged in voluntary work for the Church or other religions organisations.

The share of those engaged in voluntary work for the Church is extremely small related to the number of those, for example, who were 'peer tutors' at confirmation camp or club leaders for teenagers. All in all every fifth young adult (in the metropolitan area 22% and in Kallio 20%) had been a 'peer tutor' in their youth or a club leader in the parish. Of those who once were peer tutors at confirmation camp only one out of ten was currently engaged in voluntary work for the Church, with a further third interested in such work.

It may well be that regarding the small share of young adults engaging in voluntary activities for the Church interest and information do not meet. Many of the same respondents who reported that they were not interested in voluntary work for the Church did indeed report that they were interested in being volunteers in work with children and young people or in voluntary work among old people, handicapped people or in helping the destitute – i.e. areas which form a core part of the Church's voluntary work. In the images of the young adults these modes of action, however, are apparently not associated with the activities of the Church. The study also shows that many people might participate if only they were to be asked to join in. More than half of the young adults in the metropolitan area not involved in voluntary work reported that their non-involvement was to some extent due to the fact that they had not been asked to become volunteers.[72]

Confirmation classes as a place for asking questions and for growth

Among young Finns confirmation classes constitute a strong part of youth culture, and continue to involve almost nine out of ten young people. The figure of Finnish young people attending confirmation classes has remained at high levels over the years. The percentage of 15-year-olds attending confirmation classes was 88 percent in 2006. Every year about two thousand young people (about five percent of the confirmation class cohort) join the Church in connection with confirmation classes. In practice confirmation classes gather both young people close to the Church and also the majority of those young people whose relationship with the Church has been distant ever since childhood.[73]

---

72 Grönlund 2006.
73 Niemelä 2002; 2006c.

But did confirmation classes have any effect on the religious and spiritual lives of the young adults? Of the respondents to the telephone survey of young adults in the metropolitan area one third (30%) reported that confirmation classes had had a positive effect on their religious and spiritual lives, with one tenth (10%) reporting negative effects.[74] In Kallio the share of those reporting a positive effect was 32 per cent and a negative effect 14 per cent. The remainder estimated that confirmation classes had had no effect on their own spiritual lives. The estimated effect of confirmation classes on attitudes to the Church and the parish is described to be predominantly positive: 40 per cent describe the effect as positive, nine percent as negative. Women estimated the effect of confirmation classes to be more positive than men (p<.001).

Most of the young people now considering resignation from the Church had completed confirmation classes.[75] Those contemplating resignation had more negative experiences of confirmation classes than most (see Figure 20). For the majority of those considering resignation confirmation classes had had no effect on their spiritual lives. A considerable number of those believing themselves likely to resign from the Church, almost a quarter (23%) reported a negative effect. Only 6 per cent reported a positive effect. Among those who had already resigned from the Church and could not imagine rejoining negative effects had been even more common. Naturally confirmation classes had been experienced most positively by those who could not imagine that they would ever resign from the Church. Only three per cent of these people reported a negative effect of confirmation classes on their own spiritual lives with almost half reporting a positive effect.

---

74 Other studies report similar findings regarding the effectiveness of confirmation classes. See Niemelä 2002; 2006c.

75 Of those considering leaving the Church in Kallio almost all (97%) had
attended confirmation classes, and the same goes for those considering joining
the Church (82%).

Figure 20. Effect of confirmation classes on religious and spiritual life among young adults in the Helsinki metropolitan area on the basis of commitment to the Church (N=1,000). (Telephone Survey Young Adults in the Helsinki Metropolitan Area 2004, N=1,000) %

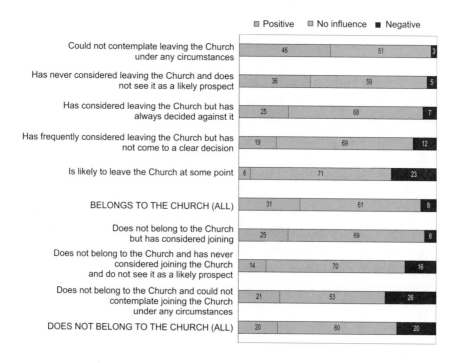

All those interviewees considering resignation from the Church had attended confirmation classes. However, they had done so driven largely by external tradition - "*and Grandma would have been very upset if I hadn't gone*" and by peer pressure. Some had actually joined the Church for that purpose in order to join their pals in confirmation classes. For many the best thing about confirmation classes was hanging out with their friends. Skiing and camping trips in Lapland, confirmation classes with riding and so on meant having fun together and a side product was that confirmation classes "consolidated friendships". They were seldom felt to have gained anything religious or spiritual. "*There wasn't much that was religious or spiritual, but I suppose it's the same for most, so it's more having fun and meeting new people.*" Some interviewees regretted this weak contribution.

"[Confirmation classes] left me once again with a somewhat really vague and somehow confusing image of the Church. At a time when I would have had most of all to ask I went off for a week of confirmation classes for that very reason and there was no listening ear or anybody who would take me seriously, only that there's somebody with the guts to have the courage of his convictions. That's what I missed, that I could have got answers to why I belong to the Church, for example, and am I a Lutheran. And then that was somehow all rejected."

In many ways confirmation classes seemed to serve as a watershed in relation to being active in the parish and in attitudes to the Church. Confirmation classes and in general the age of confirmation classes is in many ways a milestone when one's relationship with religion is contemplated and activity in the parish either increases or ceases. For those contemplating resignation from the Church and those who had already resigned confirmation classes had frequently also been a milestone with a negative effect on their own religiosity and spiritual life. Confirmation classes as an experience might be "absolutely awful". The reason was seen in part to be the values of the instructors, which were felt to be judgemental. The personality or ability of the parish workers to discuss might also cause a sense of rejection. Conversely, when the experience of confirmation classes had been positive, the parish workers treated the young people as equals and supported their own thinking. Confirmation classes were considered to have had a positive effect on one's own religiosity and spiritual life by stimulating people to think. Religious deliberations, however, might also drive them away from traditional religiosity.

Since confirmation classes come at a point in life at which identity is formed, the environment they offer for identity formation is decisive. This is the main question. In what connections can one contemplate one's own self and spiritual growth of share one's own inner life with others: one's own joy and suffering, relations to other people, the world, the environment, the supernatural, what is to come? People leave the Church most commonly between the ages of 18 and 29. At this age the results of the identity work initiated in adolescence begins to bear fruit. While in adolescence the question is "Who am I?", thinking becomes more independent and the same age is also associated by many with the experience of confirmation classes, the young person reflects the experiences gained in confirmation classes, and also from the perspective of his/her own identity – did confirmation classes equip the individual to understand the world? Those far from the Church reported ample experience according to which confirmation classes had not supported their own deliberations about life, or the understanding of Christianity or the content of Lutheranism. When considering the positive experiences of confirmation classes the subjects expressed a desire for confirmation classes which would permit one's own thinking, questioning and deliberation.

IV FROM AUTHORITARIAN RELIGIOSITY TO PERSONAL CONVICTION

From the handing down of religious beliefs to spiritual quest

The explanation for the weakening of religious institutions and the drifting of young adults away from traditional religiosity has been sought in the decline of religious education. One of the core reasons for young people being less religious in traditional sense has been seen in the fact that young people are no longer brought up to be religious as were former generations. Religiosity is no longer something to be inherited from one's parents but something to be constructed through one's own personal search. The French sociologist Danièle Hervieu-Léger calls this the breaking of the chain of memory. The countries of modern Europe are increasingly incapable of sustaining the memory which is the cornerstone of individuals' religious existence. Religion is more a matter of experience and social ties than of a tradition handed down from generation to generation. Religion nowadays, argues Hervieu-Léger, is a private matter and many parents let their children find and choose their religion for themselves irrespective of the religion of the parents. The notion of a self-selected religion puts personal experience and the authenticity of the individual's own search before the religion offered by tradition and institution.[1]

To what extent have Finns received religious upbringing in their homes? Comparison of people of different ages shows a gradual decline in religious upbringing at home. Of all Finns 66 per cent report according to the *World Values Survey 2005* that they received religious upbringing. Among pensioners 75 per cent of all Finns received religious upbringing, of those under 25 years of age, 56 per cent. The share of those receiving religious

---

1   Hervieu-Léger 2000, 123–140; 1998.

upbringing in their homes is especially low among young people and young adults in the metropolitan area. The rural way of life would appear to retain traditional religiosity much better. Of those living in rural areas more than 70 per cent of all age groups receive religious upbringing in their homes. In the metropolitan area among those under 25 years of age only every third (31%) respondent reported receiving religious upbringing in the home. The share diminishes dramatically the younger the age group concerned (see Figure 21).

Figure 21. Share of those receiving religious upbringing in the home among different age groups. (World Values 2005.) %.

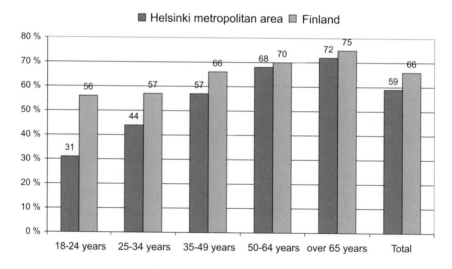

According to the telephone interviews less than half (46%) of young adults aged 20–39 both in the whole metropolitan area and in Kallio felt they had received religious upbringing as children (see Table 9). The younger the respondent the smaller the share receiving religious upbringing. Among those under 30 years old 42 per cent reported receiving religious upbringing, among those over 30 years old 50 per cent.[2]

---

2   The same difference in age groups can be seen in the results of the Youth Barometer on religiosity in the homes of those ages 15–29. Uskon asia 2006, 69.

The person giving the religious upbringing was generally the child's mother or grandmother, from whom every second young adult reported receiving religious upbringing. Only one out of four (27%) had received religious upbringing from their fathers. If the father had given religious upbringing in the family, the mother had almost always also been active in it. Only two per cent of young adults reported receiving religion upbringing from their fathers but not from their mothers. Only one out of five mentions a godparent as giving religious upbringing even though the child's religious upbringing is thought to be the main task of godparents.

Table 9. Young adults in the metropolitan area and religious upbringing in the home. (Telephone Survey Young Adults in the Helsinki Metropolitan Area 2004, N=1,000)

Have been taught an evening prayer at home	67 %
Have had a religious upbringing as a child	46 %
From whom did you get a religious upbringing as a child?	
Mother	50 %
Father	27 %
(Both parents	25%)
Godparent	18 %
Grandmother	47 %
Grandfather	16 %
A teacher at school	77 %

Every fourth (25%) respondent had received religious upbringing from both parents. Of those resigning from the Church only 13 per cent had received religious upbringing from both their fathers and their mothers. Every fourth had received religious upbringing from only one parent and two out of three from neither of the parents. Of those belonging to the Church every fourth (25%) had received religious upbringing from both parents and every third (31%) from one parent.

What then does the religious upbringing given at home contain? In the present study young adults were only asked whether or not they felt there had been religious upbringing in their homes, but not about the content of such upbringing. Some response to the question is available from the Youth Barometer Survey of 2006, to which 1,900 young Finns aged 15 to 29 responded. These young people and young adults described the religiosity of their homes as follows:

We talked about religion in my childhood home: 53%

We respected the day of rest: 38%

The children attended Sunday school: 37%

We said grace before eating: 14%

We attended church regularly: 11%

We had prayers at home: 6%.[3]

Most of the young adults in the metropolitan area and in Kallio were involved in one way or another in Church activities as children or as young people (see Table 10). Of young adults living in the metropolitan area and also specifically in Kallio nine out of ten had attended confirmation classes. Two respondents out of three have been involved in day clubs or Sunday school and almost half in youth clubs. Every fourth has participated in Church youth groups and every fifth has been a peer tutor in confirmation classes.

Table 10. Participation in Church activities as a child and in youth among young adults in the Helsinki metropolitan area and in Kallio. (Telephone Survey Young Adults in the Helsinki Metropolitan Area 2004, N=1,000; Telephone Survey Young Adults in Kallio 2004, N=500.)

	Helsinki metropolitan area	Kallio
Has attended Sunday school or Church day clubs	69 %	69 %
Has attended Church boys'/girls' clubs	42 %	43 %
Has attended Church youth groups	26 %	22 %
Has been a peer tutor at confirmation classes	22 %	20 %
Has taken confirmation classes	89 %	90 %
N	1000	500

Overall the majority of the young adults do indeed to some extent have backgrounds with elements of religion and church

---

3   Uskon asia 2006, 70–71.

orientation, and many of them had had at least some form of religious education. But does religious upbringing and education have any significance at the stage when young adults are building their own independent lives?

Research on religiosity among Finns, the present study included, shows that many young adults, especially men, are indifferent to religion. The research shows that fewer and fewer urban Finns had a religious upbringing in childhood. To what extent can religious attitudes be explained by religious upbringing in childhood? And where can religious attitudes be accounted for by various demographic considerations such as gender, age, place of residence, family situation and the duration of residence in the metropolitan area? This was scrutinised using stepwise regression analysis of the data obtained through the telephone interviews with young adults (see Table 11). The explanatory variable was the individual's view of the importance of religion/faith in his/her life.

Table 11. Factors explaining the importance of religion/faith in the entire metropolitan area among those aged 20-39. Stepwise regression analysis. N=1,000, R=.391, R2= 0.153 Adj R2=0.149.F=34.41***. (Telephone Survey Young Adults in the Helsinki Metropolitan Area 2004, N=1,000)

	B	Beta	t	p
(Constant)	2.28		10.04	<.001
Has had a religious upbringing	0.73	0.29	9.63	<.001
Number of children	0.12	0.10	2.87	<.001
Years of residence in Helsinki area	-0.14	-0.15	-4.69	<.001
Gender	-0.27	-0.11	-3.63	<.001
Age	0.02	0.10	3.08	.002

The factor emerging as the most powerful explanatory variable for religious attitude was religious upbringing in childhood. Other statistically significant explanatory variables were gender, age, number of own children, duration of residence in the metropolitan area. These factors explained 15 per cent of the individual's current attitude to religion. The younger the individual and the greater the duration of residence in the metropolitan area the less importance was attached to religion. On the other hand, if the respondent had children and was a woman, the more likely she was to attach importance to religion. However, the factor by far most significant among all of these was whether or not the respondent had received religious upbringing in childhood. Almost half (40%) of the young adults who had had religious upbringing in their homes considered faith important part of their life. Of those young adults in whose homes there had been on religious upbringing only 15 per cent considered religion an important part of their lives.[4]

The influence of religious upbringing in the home was particularly strong when both father and mother had been actively involved. This is obvious, for example, when the religious identity of the young adults is considered. Seventy-two percent of those who have had a religious upbringing from both of parents regard themselves as religious, while 52 percent of those who have had a religious upbringing from only one parent and 27 percent of those who have had a religious upbringing from neither of the parents do so.

The Youth Barometer survey 2006 also shows that religiosity in the home was closely connected to a young adult's religiosity. There was also a strong connection between the age of the parents and the religiosity of the home: the earlier the parents of the respondent had been born, the more religious the respondent considered the parental home to have been.[5]

If we then consider the significance of a religious upbringing in childhood or youth for subsequent participation in Church activities the regular participation learned in childhood and youth is important. Active churchgoers among young adults are typically those who ever since childhood have grown into the Church through its work with children and young people. Participation in youth groups in the parish is particularly significant. It is extremely rare for young adults to "find" the Church and faith after a childhood and youth spent far from the Church.

There is also a significant connection between whether a young person has had a religious upbringing at home and how that young person feels about confirmation classes (p $\leq$.001). Those young people who consider themselves to have had a religious

4   Niemelä 2006d.
5   Uskon asia 2006, 71.

upbringing typically report positive experiences of confirmation classes. Altogether 40 per cent of the young adults in the metropolitan area reporting having had a religious upbringing reported a positive effect of confirmation classes on their religious and spiritual lives. On the other hand, of those young people in whose homes there was no religious upbringing only a fifth (22%) reported a positive effect of confirmation classes on their religious and spiritual lives. Experiences during confirmation classes and religious upbringing in the home are both of great significance in subsequent commitment to the Church among young adults.

Figure 22. Reactions to the statement "there is only one true religion" among young adults in the Helsinki metropolitan area receiving religious upbringing from both parents, one parent or neither parent. (Telephone Survey Young Adults in the Helsinki Metropolitan Area 2004, N=1,000.) %.

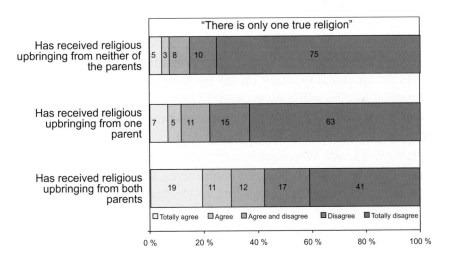

There is also a strong connection between religious upbringing and how a young adult relates to religions and the truth they profess. Those young adults in whose homes there had been no religious upbringing are extremely relativistic and ambivalent towards religious beliefs. Of those young people neither of whose parents had provided religious upbringing three quarters (75%) totally disagreed with the statement "there is only one try religions" (see

107

Figure 22). Of those who had had religious upbringing from one or other of their parents two thirds (63%) totally disagreed with the statement. Of those who had had religious upbringing from both parents those totally disagreeing with the statement amounted to well under half (41%).[6]

A metamorphosis of religion

The decline of the traditional religious institutions in Finland and also elsewhere in western Europe has not meant that the supernatural dimension has in some sense vanished from life. Many researchers of religion mention a *metamorphosis* of religion rather than a decline. For example, the German sociologist Thomas Luckmann claims that people are as religious today as they ever were, but religion now has a different meaning than before in their social lives.[7] In the examination of the change in religiosity among Finns and also of young urban people it is obvious that although there has been a decline in the institutional forms of religion, this has not led to an overall decline in religion.

In international research on the sociology of religion increasing attention has recently been paid to the growth of spirituality.[8] According to numerous studies more and more people are calling themselves spiritual rather than religious. According to Paul Heelas and Linda Woodhead (2005) among others, more and more people are inclined to describe themselves as spiritual and fewew and fewer as religious. According to Heelas and Woodhead in so doing they turn in on themselves and seek for a purpose of life there. People are reluctant to commit to hierarchies, an omniscient institution and would rather have freedom to grow and develop as their own unique selves instead of going to churches and submitting themselves to their teaching.[9]

---

6   Pearson Chi-Square 99.43***.
7   Luckmann 1967.
8   See e.g. Heelas 2002; Moberg 2002; Roof 2003; Heelas & Woodhead 2005.
9   Heelas & Woodhead 2005.

In their book *Spiritual Revolution* (2005) Heelas and Woodhead write that our age is characterised by a massive subjective turn in modern culture. This refers to the rejection of a life defined by external or objective roles and obligations towards something that is primarily defined by the individual's own subjective experiences and feelings. Choices in life are based less on external expectations. Rather they emanate from the individual's own personal feelings, desires, abilities and personal needs. Nor do people primarily conceive of themselves as a member of some community and as a link in the chain of tradition. Life is rather based increasingly on the individual's own subjective feelings. Life is not dictated by external authorities; the aim is to be more and more the supreme authority of one's own life. The endeavour is not to follow readymade models for life, but to seek for an internally guided and optimally unique life and to break free as far as possible from dependence on others' knowledge and wisdom and become "one's own true self". Then the most important value in life is an authentic connection to one's own inner self, not a life in keeping with external authorities.[10]

In the religious field this change inevitably leads to breaking away from the forms of religiosity which are based on hierarchy. It also leads to religiosity being increasingly the individual's own choice. People do not belong to the Church or religious organisations because they were brought up in that tradition. Membership and participation must be in line with the individual's own personal thinking and opinions.

The Swedish Ann Aldén on the basis of several extensive empirical religiosity studies has compiled a summary of religiosity and spirituality and of the change occurring in the field.[11] This analysis is not coloured by values, thus it does not claim that the development is good or bad, but describes the ongoing change. The direction of change is from left to right, from religiosity to spirituality:

---

10   Heelas & Woodhead 2005, 2–4; Inglehart 1997.
11   Aldén 2005.; see also Alden 2006.

RELIGIOSITY	SPIRITUALITY
God beyond	God within
We are sinners and need forgiveness	We are wounded and need healing
Fulfilment of duty	Self-fulfilment
Jesus/God as Lord and King	Jesus/God as Friend and Life
Word-Sermon-Understanding	Mystery-Eucharist-Experience
Faith as truth	Faith as trust
The narrow gate	The wide embrace
Go to heaven	Live on earth
Philosophical truth (I claim…)	Psychological truth (I feel…)
Hierarchical authority	Experiential authority
Hard boundaries - exclusivism	Soft boundaries - inclusivism
Command - Obey	Empower-create
Hierarchical relations	Mutual relations

In Aldén's analysis religiosity is highly individualistic, experiential, non-authoritarian, non-dogmatic and within the individual. This new form of religiosity perhaps renders comprehensible why the religious upbringing of one's own children is found to be difficult and even troublesome. For modern people religion is not something that can be poured over another person from outside; it is within the person. It is not habits, what is held true or respect for authority, not something to be learned but only experienced.[12]

Numerous scholars have argued that we live in an age in which the traditional forms of religion, especially Christianity, are giving way to novel forms.[13] Modern people are interested in the various dimensions of spirituality but not in the traditions of the Church. Then religion is seen to be bound to tradition and institutions, whereas spirituality is seen as contemplation of self and inner existentialism and concentration on experiences and in the breakthrough of the eastern cultural sphere.[14] Compared to the previous generation the new generations do a great deal of work in

---

12   Majamäki 2006, 332–341.

13   Among others Robert Wuthnow in his work *After Heaven* describes this as seeker-oriented spirituality. The culture of spiritual seeking is also discussed by Roof (see e.g. Roof 2003), likewise Paul Heelas and Linda Woodhead in *Spiritual Revolution* (2005).

14   In the field of science this change is conceptualised as a new period in religion and spirituality (Hunt 2005, 22) and the division between religiosity and Church religiosity has disappeared. See also Moberg 2002, 138.

order to arrive at their own view of life, the religiosity of the older generations was more guaranteed and received as given. Whereas earlier the personal life was subjugated to the higher power, nowadays the cultivation of the individual and his/her own life has become sacrosanct.[15] Spirituality refers now to what was referred to as religion in the broadest and non-traditional sense. Then religion has to do with the purpose of life and making sense. This was a kind of religiosity above religions or implicit religiosity.[16] This culture of spiritual quest is so powerful that we can even say that in the west we are heading for the greatest spiritual revolution since the Reformation.

The religious identity of young adults is characterised by an overall greater openness than among other age groups. It is obvious that young adults do not want to identify themselves as followers of a specific religious institution, but are more likely to identify themselves as religious or spiritual in a looser and more open sense. This trend is very obvious when comparing their identity as Lutherans and Christians with older age groups in Finland. Young adults in both rural and urban areas do not tend to identify themselves notably as often as Lutherans as they identify themselves as Christians. Only 50 percent of young adults identify themselves as Lutherans while 74 percent identify themselves as Christians.[17] The difference is the greater the younger the age group in question: of those aged 15–24 only 44 per cent consider themselves to be Lutherans, however, 75 per cent consider themselves Christians. In urban areas the difference is greater than in rural areas: young urban people are much inclined to describe

15   Heelas & Woodhead 2005.

16   Erich Fromm (1986, 27) among others means by religion "any model of thought or action shared by a certain group of people which gives a direction to their lives and something to which they can dedicate themselves." According to Fromm (1986, 31) every individual has a need for religion, the need finds the frame of reference and something to which a person can surrender. Smart (2005, 12) mentions "religiosity above religions", when a person has a profound spiritual dimension without belonging to any movement or organisation or that there is some transcendental influence in his/her life. A person may perceive the ultimate spiritual significance, for example through communion with Nature or relations to other people. Such religiosity has been described as implicit religiosity. Gollnick 2005, 19–20.

17   These figures are based on the Church Monitor 2004 survey.

themselves as Christians but not as Lutherans. Among older age groups (40+) the proportion of those who identify themselves as Christians (78%) is only a little higher than the proportion of those who identify themselves as Lutherans (74%). Among those over 65 there is actually a larger number of those who regard themselves as Lutheran (86%) than of those who regard themselves as Christian (81%). This discrepancy also reflects the differences in orientation of different age groups to the Lutheran Church and membership as discussed earlier.

Young adults also prefer to describe themselves as spiritual rather than as religious. Of the young people in the metropolitan area 69 per cent consider themselves spiritual, and 45 per cent consider themselves religious. Among those who have resigned from the Church the corresponding figures are 73 and 21 per cent. Of those belonging to the Church 46 per cent considered themselves religious and 64 per cent spiritual.

When the two main aspects of religious identity – religious and spiritual – are crosstabulated we come out with four groups among urban young adults (see Table 12): those who identify themselves as

1) "religious and spiritual" (with 37% of urban young adults identifying themselves as such)

2) "religious but non-spiritual" (8%)

3) "spiritual but non-religious" (34%)

4) "non-religious – non-spiritual" (21%).

Table 12. Religious identity of young adults in Helsinki metropolitan area. (Telephone Survey Young Adults in the Helsinki Metropolitan Area 2004, N=1,000.)

	SPIRITUAL	NON-SPIRITUAL	Total
RELIGIOUS	37% (Religious and spiritual)	8% (Religious, non-spiritual)	45%
NON-RELIGIOUS	34% (Spiritual, non-religious)	21% (Non-religious, non-spiritual)	55%
Total	69%	31%	100%

When discussing what is religious and what is spiritual we get into linguistic difficulties: What do people mean when they use these terms? What does it mean to be spiritual or religious or both or neither of these? Clarity in this can be achieved by scrutinising differences in religious attitudes between those who identify themselves as religious or spiritual or both/neither. How do these people differ from each other? These four groups are next examined more closely.

1. *Religious and spiritual* (37%) respondents are more likely to be female. 44 percent of urban young females identify themselves as such and 31 percent of males. They have typically not lived in the Helsinki metropolitan area all their lives and are likely to be more than 30 years old. They are more common among those with children than without and most common among those who are at home with their children. They typically regard faith and religion as a somewhat or quite an important part of their lives. They most actively seek different parts to their worldview from different sources and are most interested in buying spiritual literature. They tend to subscribe at some level to typical Christian beliefs. Of the four groups they are most likely to believe in supernatural phenomena like ghosts and superstition. They typically belong to the Evangelical Lutheran Church (82%) or some other denomination (10%). They are typically active or quite active in their private and public religious activities.

2. *Religious – non-spiritual* (8%) respondents are clearly the smallest group among the urban young adults. Only 6 percent of males and 9 percent of females identify themselves as religious, but not as spiritual. They are most often found among those who have lived in Helsinki metropolitan area only for a short while. Among them, the role of institutional religion is strongest and they are least interested in alternative religious movements. They are most often members of a church, 87 percent belong to the Evangelical Lutheran Church, 8 percent to another denomination. Only 5 percent do not belong to any denomination. Out of the four groups they agree most with Christian belief statements. They are typically active or fairly active in their private and public religious practices. Out of the four groups, they are most likely to think that there is only one true religion in the world. They typically regard faith and religion as a very or quite important part of their life.

3. *Spiritual – non-religious* (34%) respondents form the second largest group among young urban adults with 34 percent of males

and 33 percent of females. They are most typically under 30 years and have lived in Helsinki metropolitan area for more than 20 years or all their lives. They are passive in their religious observance and are most in disagreement with a statement that there is only one true religion. They typically disagree with Christian belief statements or deem them unlikely. 26 percent of them are not members of any religious organisation, while 74 percent belong to the Evangelical Lutheran Church. Faith and religion do not play a big role in their lives: most of them regard these as totally or somewhat unimportant.

4. *Non-spiritual – non-religious* (21%) respondents are clearly least interested in all kinds of spiritual and religious matters. They account for 29 percent among males and 14 percent of females. They are most common among those who have lived in Helsinki metropolitan area for more than 20 years or all their lives. They are very doubtful about the existence of God or any kind of higher force. They typically disagree with all kinds of belief statements. They are extremely passive in their private religious observance, but still one fourth of them have attended church within the last 12 months. Even though they are religiously very passive, 77 percent are still members of a religious organisation, mostly of the Evangelical Lutheran Church.

The examination above shows that the differences between those identifying themselves as religious and/or spiritual adhere to the very same line typically in use in research in the sociology of religion. For those identifying themselves as only religious the role of institutional religiosity is strongest. On the other hand those identifying themselves as spiritual and religious are most open to alternative religious movements. The relationship to religion of those identifying themselves as only spiritual is the most relativistic and they believe least of all that there is only one religion that can purvey the truth.

Those young adults considering resignation from the Church very seldom described themselves as religious; less than one fifth of these reported that they were religious (see Table 13). However, the majority of them (62%) described themselves as spiritual.

Table 13. Young adults in the Helsinki metropolitan area identifying themselves as religious or spiritual on the basis of commitment to the Church. (Telephone Survey Young Adults in the Helsinki Metropolitan Area 2004.) %.

	Religious	Spiritual	N
Could not contemplate leaving the Church under any circumstances	70	61	168
Has never considered leaving the Church and does not see it as a likely prospect	50	69	303
Has considered leaving the Church but has always decided against it	41	64	137
Has considered leaving the Church and may resign	18	62	173
Does not belong to the Church and has considered joining	52	74	50
Does not belong to the Church and has not considered joining	33	58	67
Does not belong to the Church and could not imagine joining	27	61	96
Total	43	64	994

The same emphasis on spirituality was also discernible in the interviews with those who had resigned from the Church. All the men who had left the Church and who were interviewed for the study reported that genuine and real spirituality makes its appearance apart from religions. It emanates from the individual himself and its manifestations are not limited by official beliefs or behavioural norms. One of the interviewees described spirituality as a personal relationship focussed on other people and higher power. Its personal nature requires that no institution or organisation has defined the quality or forms of manifestation in advance.[18]

Although those on the edge of Church membership do not often seek answers among the traditional articles of faith and institutions, they are nevertheless preoccupied by spiritual issues.[19]

---

18 Kosunen 2006, 270.

19 The view of the American social scientist Ronald Inglehart (1997, 8–23, 74–90, 280–285) among others is that the position of religion today is as follows: According to Inglehart in the new world view earthly authorities appealing to reason are not preferred, likewise absolute rules and traditional religious values. However, this does not mean that people are totally alienated from spiritual questions. According to Inglehart spiritual questions actually preoccupy people more. Modern people contemplate life and its purpose more than before. But the individual so contemplating does not set out to seek answers in traditional religions or institutions. The existence of spiritual needs is also born

Many interviewees wanted to point this out. Many of them felt a spiritual yearning, but this finds expression in new ways, where thinking combines different religiosity of spirituality with science and rationality. This is the post secularisation characteristic of the modern age.[20] In postsecular thinking there is no denial of religion or spirituality, nor yet of science and rationality. In practice this is tolerance of many explanations and conflicting phenomena, where the religions solution is not adhered to nor is refuge sought in "logical" solutions. Life is granted an element of mystery and myth, which cannot necessarily be converted into rationality.[21]

Examination of the spiritual profile of young adults also shows that even though most young adults find the institutional religiosity represented by the Church to be alien and distant, for them spiritual values understood broadly are important and spiritual sensitivity can be found in them. The young adults living in Kallio yearn for quiet in the midst of haste, experiences of mystery and beauty as a counterbalance to rational thought and deliberation of values in the search for the purpose of life. Communality is also important, especially the promotion of peace. Such spirituality is more common among women than among men.[22]

The analysis of religious and spiritual identity above has shown that an individual's identity differs along with many demographic variables. Women nearing 40 having only lived a short time in the metropolitan area consider themselves more frequently religious than younger people, those who have lived longer in the metropolitan area and men. But what are the issues that really matter? Sequential logistic regression analysis was run to visualize the demographic issues with the greatest effect on respondent's

---

out by empirical studies. See for example Inglehart & Baker 2000, 47–49; Mikkola 2003, 228–229.

20   The concept endeavours to make a distinction from traditional secularisation theories in which science and religion are conceived of as opposites and in which religion is assumed to be dying out as societies modernise. The concept endeavours to make a distinction also from the new agenda of describing the religiosity of the new age because the use of conception of new age is very varied and refers to very different beliefs and values.

21   Cf. Vattimo 1999, 122.

22   Tirri 2006, 299–303.

religious and spiritual identity (whether an individual regards him/herself as religious/spiritual or not). The analysis (see Table 14) shows that gender, years of residence in Helsinki metropolitan area and age are all issues that have a statistically significant effect on respondent's religious identity. Women, those who have lived in the area a short while and those who are older are most likely to regard themselves as religious. Demographic variables studied explain 10.2 percent of individual's religious identity. However, when it comes to spiritual identity demographic issues explain only 3.6 percent. Gender is the only factor that has a statistically significant effect. Women are more likely to identify themselves as spiritual.

Table 14. Demographic variables affecting religious and spiritual identity. Logistic regression analysis (method enter). (Telephone Survey Young Adults in the Helsinki Metropolitan Area 2004, N=1,000)

	REGARDS HIM/HERSELF AS RELIGIOUS		REGARDS HIM/HERSELF AS SPIRITUAL	
	B	Wald	B	Wald
Gender	.61	18.28***	.62	15.93***
Years of residence in Helsinki area	.35	38.10***	.08	1.79
Has children	-.29	2.75	-.17	.81
Age	-.22	8.27**	.01	.01
Working	-.19	.09	.59	.77
Housewife	-.32	.21	1.14	2.42
Student	-.36	.30	.30	.19
Unemployed	.02	.00	.37	.23
Constant	-.25	.14	.-1.93	7.19**
R^2	.102		.036	

But when it comes to religious and spiritual identity, what is the meaning of religious upbringing? As noted above, religious upbringing is closely connected to the role of religion in the lives of young adults. The same goes for religious identity: only 29 percent of those with no religious upbringing at home regard themselves as religious, while 64 percent of those who have had a religious upbringing do so. However, spiritual identity seems to develop very independently without the active influence of religious upbringing: almost the same amount (66%) of those with no religious upbringing at home regard themselves as spiritual as those who have had a religious upbringing (75%).

Sequential logistic regression analysis was run in order to analyse the co-effect of various forms of religious education on respondents' religious and spiritual identity (whether an individual regards him/herself as religious and spiritual or not) to examine which influences really matter. Model 1 shows the effects of various influences on whether an individual regards him/herself as religious or not (see Table 15). Of the different sources of religious upbringing elicited parents are the most influential mediators of religion and religious identity. Grandmother comes next. A schoolteacher, a godparent and grandfather as sources of religious upbringing seem to be rather irrelevant when it comes to the religious identity of an individual. Of various forms of Church child and youth activities attendance at Church Sunday school or day clubs and most of all Church youth groups are most influential. In all, when it comes to religious identity the sequential logistic regression analysis shows that the influences of a mother and a father and attending Church youth activities are the most powerful.

Model 2 shows the effects of various forms of religious education on one's spiritual identity. The results are very different than those found in the analysis of the effect of religious upbringing on religious identity. The data shows that the effects of religious upbringing are very limited when it comes to spiritual identity.

Table 15. Logistic regression analysis (method enter) on influences on religious identity of young adults in the Helsinki Metropolitan Area (*Do you regard yourselves as religious/spiritual or not?*). (Telephone Survey Young Adults in the Helsinki Metropolitan Area 2004, N=1,000)

	Model 1: RELIGIOUS IDENTITY		Model 2: SPIRITUAL IDENTITY	
	B	Wald	B	Wald
Has had religious upbringing from her/his mother	.79	12.28***	.12	.56
…from a father	.77	17.10***	.31	2.76+
…from a godparent	.24	1.53	.06	.10
…from a grandmother	.36	5.47*	.12	.70
…from a grandfather	-.02	.01	.22	1.02
Has had religious education from a teacher at school	-.37	4.74*	.24	2.20
Has attended Sunday school or Church day clubs	.30	3.33*	.06	.17
Has attended Church boys'/girls' clubs	.10	.46	-.08	.31
Has attended Church youth groups	.73	14.04***	.32	2.66
Has worked as a Church group leader	.29	2.00	-.32	.006
Has attended confirmation classes	-.23	.86	-.29	1.54
Constant	-1.13	18.95***	.35	1.99
R^2	.227		.033	

All in all, religious identity seems to be very dependent on religious upbringing. However, spiritual identity has very little to do with religious upbringing. For young adults *spirituality* is obviously not something to do with tradition – and therefore with religious upbringing and education, but only with one's personal relationship with transcendence. The study shows that spirituality has become complex seeking in which the individual seeks him/herself [23], and in this searching there is reliance on one's own discretion[24], not on some "truth" inherited from earlier generations.

---

23   Wuthnow 1998, 2.
24   Smart 2005, 604.

V SUMMARY OF FINDINGS AND DISCUSSION

This study set out to increase and disseminate knowledge and understanding of the lives and life situations of new generations of Finns and their values and religiosity. An effort was also made with their help to understand the special features of today and form an idea of the direction in which the religious attitudes are most probably also developing in other sections of the population. The focus of the empirical study was the new generations, those aged 20–39 resident in the metropolitan area and especially in the Kallio district of Helsinki.

The research project addresses the metropolitan area and especially the Kallio district, since the relative share of young adults in the population is high and migration frequent. The age group of young adults is prominent there among those who have resigned from the Church. The Kallio neighbourhood is an area of young adults with its own special characteristics, and researching it yields a great deal of information about the lives of young adults in general. A strong migration flow means that Kallio is a district of transition, for many the gateway to Helsinki. Indeed, Kallio is something of a cradle of urban life – Kallio urbanises many of the young Finnish adults.

The young adults of the metropolitan area and especially those of Kallio can also be considered an ideological and religious core or even *avant garde* through whom new ideals spread to the rest of the population, and this includes religion. This being so, it may be assumed that the nature of religiosity there will provide an indication of the forthcoming development in other sections of the life.

The study is based on extensive empirical research data. The main sources are telephone interview data from 500 young adults aged 20–39 living in the Kallio district of Helsinki and the telephone interview data from 1,000 of their peers living in the metropolitan area (Helsinki, Espoo, Vantaa). These findings are compared to extensive data covering the whole of Finland. The researchers on the project also interviewed more than 100 individuals face-to-face.

We refer to the new generations (1964–1984), i.e. those now aged 20–39 as young adults. The first part of young adulthood, emerging adulthood, the years between 18 and 25 are shown by the research to be a time for concentrating strongly on oneself. It is also a time of many changes, identity experiments and uncertainties. It is living in an interim state on the way to an adulthood assumed to be characterised by stability and a responsible way of life. The way of life typical of emerging adulthood describes the living reality of more and older individuals, especially in the developed West and there specifically in the urban areas. Youth is prolonged to more than thirty or even forty years, and the way of life it typifies may be reverted to at a later stage in life. This extended urban youth has come to constitute a sort of new middle class, who are the first to take innovations onboard and pass them on to others.

The life of an urban young adult is an active stage typified by career development geared to one's own interest and by a postponement of family life. Our study showed that friends and acquaintances are important, likewise self-fulfilment and an orientation towards entertainment. Many people could not find anything less interesting than religious or political institutions and the inherent guidelines as to how life should be lived and how one ought to act in society. Urban young adults represent that section of the population which is very mobile and lives an active life.

Urban young adults stress the freedom of the individual, are self-directed and pursue authenticity. The contemplation of one's own inner self characteristic of emerging adulthood was common, likewise concentration on oneself. This was manifest in the talk of the young adults in expressions of justification of things departing from the self – that things either were, or were not "something for me". Pondering "what I really want" and "I can become what I really am" was common. Such definition of objectives and way of life through oneself had been considered an inevitable developmental trend in our culture.[1] In this we cannot turn back the clock.[2] Life is constant identity work and what today is "something for me" may not be so tomorrow.

The culture of self-fulfilment, normativity of the individual and of authenticity appearing among young adults is driving them away from Church membership. If the Church is not perceived to be "something for me" and as a community to whose values one can subscribe, the tendency to leave the Church is strong. Reasons for being a member of the Church are personal and the Church is required to provide meaningfulness from one's own personal perspective on life. The thinking prevailing among the older generations that belonging to the Church is a part of being Finnish and part of the Finnish way of life is seldom found among the younger generation. Doubts are being cast on the meaningfulness of belonging to the Church and participating in its activities. All in all the share of young people in the metropolitan area and especially in Kallio with a strong commitment to Church membership is small and conversely there are more than elsewhere living on the edge of Church membership or totally outside the Church.

For approximately every fourth young adult faith and religion were at least a fairly important part of life. For every tenth young adult it is extremely important. However, many young adults in practice had no connection with the Church and the Church for them was remote and indifferent. For many the relation to the Church was something from which they derived nothing. This fairly tenuous bond was supported by the fact that the existence of the Church does not intrude on the young adults' lives. Being a

---

1   Taylor 1995, 109–110.
2   Thomas Ziehe speaks of this developmental trend as an aberration of tradition affecting the way in which people understand and interpret themselves. According to Ziehe, the crumbling of the great Christian religions as the guiding light of life and the everyday, the change in sexual morals and sexual behaviour, the dismantling of gender roles, the problematisation of gender roles, the flouting of traditional work ethics and the changed attitudes to so-called authority figures are an aberration from tradition. Ziehe 1991, 17. See also Beck 1995, 12–13, 27–29. This development casts doubt on the notion of an identity for the whole of one's life. Identity is no longer felt to be something assumed and kept for life. Rather identities are tried out, altered, embellished. Ziehe 1991, 27.

member made no greater demands than payment of Church taxes. A large part of the young adults only come face to face with the Church in the course of the year through the performance of church rites. Over two thirds of them had participated in these once a year. About half of the young adults attended Church services less than once a year or in recent years not at all. Less than a tenth (4% of the young adults in Kallio and 7% in the metropolitan area) participated in religious occasions at least once a month. Participation in other religious events was even lower. Praying and reading the parish magazine was reasonably common, but reading the Bible, listening to religious programmes on the radio and listening to sacred music was rare.

Young people are open to changes, appreciate fun and enjoyment in life. From this standpoint stable Church members with traditional beliefs are perceived as unauthentic and bogged down in the old. The Church represents the everyday boredom of life. Young adults take their own lives seriously and ambitiously, and will not be content with the greyness of the everyday lives of the older generation. For many the Church and its rites represent admiration of this greyness. Even many young adults who are committed to the Church and consider religion important think that the Church seems remote and that there would be a great deal of room for improvement.

Other aspects in need of improvement were found. Urban young adults frequently think that there is no place for them and their liberal and tolerant views in the Church. Although young urban adults are liberally minded and stress enjoyment, they are not selfish egoists. Personal life projects and authenticity are not achieved at the expense of other people and nature. Human rights and animal rights are important to young adults. Indeed, human rights are so important to them that this alienates them from the Church because they feel that the Church does not promote human rights in the best possible way. This achieved its extreme manifestation in subjects' talk about the ordination of women and attitudes to homosexuality and in images of the position of the Church on these issues. The young adults were particularly critical of the Church when it appeared intolerant and old-fashioned in its attitudes. Religion and the Church are even perceived to be impedimenta on the journey towards global values in which the obligations laid on people are accompanied by obligations towards the environment.

In exaggeration one might state that young adults considered Church an uninteresting and boring institution which serves largely as a sort of support structure in life from which it was imagined that help was forthcoming in difficult situations. Despite the various criticisms, most of the young adults still belonged to the Church and in spite of considering resignation still felt some attraction to it. Frequently the Church institution was supported because the Church was seen as a bastion of spiritual values in the modern world and at best it was considered an ethical, moral and practical support. The core message of Christianity, love of one's neighbour, was appreciated among the young adults. Thus young adults are not actually anti-Church. Less than one tenth of the young adults belonging to the Church were negative or very negative about it.

What attracts people about the Church or holds them is the humanitarian work it accomplishes, the spiritual care and its involvement in turning points in life. All these serve to support communality. The young adults expressed interest in communality with a low threshold, which is broadminded, requires little commitment and is experiential. There would be considerably more interest in participating in Church activities than at present. However, the Church, too, is expected to enable a loose commitment. It is also expected that a young adult could commit on his/her own terms and even when making a commitment continue to be his/her own self. In the eyes of many young adults, the Church as it is today did not appear to be such an open-minded and tolerant organisation that they could consider it unconditionally a support structure for their lives. Their love of their fellow men and their possible relationship to God appeared to acquire a more natural expression outside the Church institution.

The majority of the young adults took a relative attitude to religious tradition and felt that there is no one true religion. The young adults moreover made a distinction between spirituality and religiosity and preferred to see themselves as spiritual rather than as religious, or then as both. The opposite of spirituality was seen to be authoritarian and dogmatic Church religion. They want to break away from this. Such s trend is obvious in many Western countries. According to Woodhead and Heelas (2005) more and more people describe themselves as "spiritual", fewer as "religious" and, as they do so, they are turning away from the Christian Church, with its rules and "self last" philosophy, and looking inwards for the meaning of life. It is a shift away from a hierarchical, all-knowing institution and a move towards having the freedom to grow and develop as a unique person rather than going to church and being led. The urban living environment itself appears in the findings of the study to be a particularly challenging area for traditional, hierarchical religion. The longer a young adult had lived in the metropolitan area, the weaker was the tie to traditional, institutional religiosity. On the other hand in relation to spirituality in a broader sense those living in the urban environment did not differ from others as being less spiritual.

The religious and spiritual attitudes of the young people reflects a change in our culture extensively evident. The orientalisation of the West is typical for our time: there has been a shift from the monotheism of the hereafter to the sanctification of the here and now. The rise of the new spirituality turns its gaze from the transcendental God to the individual him/herself. This new type of spirituality, which seems to find a connection to traditional religiosity, emerges strongly in the present research. Thinking which stresses individuality prefers internal and humanistic religion over external and authoritarian religion; the cultivation of the individual and his/her life has become sacrosanct.

All in all, the young adults are likely to describe their religious identity more openly than older age groups. They are not only likely to identify themselves as spiritual, but not as religious, but also as Christians but not as Lutherans, even though they are members of Lutheran Church. Thus, they do not want to commit themselves to any religious organisation or to describe their religiosity in terms of a religious institution. Young adults do not generally consider religious institutions necessary for their own faith. Faith is seen as a personal matter which needs no hierarchical structures. The critical attitude to institutions does not

125

only appear in the relation to the Church, but also in attitudes to other traditional institutions.

Faith and spirituality are deeply personal matters. Against such a background it is easy to understand why it is first and foremost young adults who easily resign from the Church: A rigid institution felt to be old-fashioned taking care of things which pertain to the individual alone does not make sense. Given that young adulthood is a time for concentrating strongly on oneself also renders comprehensible why many young adults find that the Church has no meaning: The meaningfulness of the Church is held up against one's own life situation in particular and against one's own values. The wider cultural significance of the Church receives less attention in the young adults' contemplations. The main reason for respondents to leave the Church was that the Church has no meaning for me. Only after this come Church taxation and disappointments with the stands taken by the Church, its actions and its employees. Other religious organisations or moving the place of residence did not in the opinions of the respondents have any effect on the matter.

The young adults are reluctant to act contrary to their own values. This can be seen that they do not want to be members of the Church if the Church is seen to represent values which a young adult cannot accept. Many young adults also do not wish to belong to the Church if they do not believe in its teachings. Even if the Church is perceived as a good organisation necessary in many ways, many young adults feel they cannot belong if they cannot commit to the spiritual message and values of the Church. The young people are no longer willing to *"belong without believing"* – the term in which Finnish and Nordic religiosity and church membership are often been described.[3]

The experience of confirmation classes is a clear watershed which may subsequently lead to resignation from the Church – the experiences of confirmation classes among those resigning from the Church were significantly more negative or meaningless than those of young adults committed to the Church. Of all the young

---

3   See eg. Davie 2000; cf. Davie 1994.

adults who had gone through confirmation classes about half felt that these classes had had no effect whatsoever on their religious or spiritual lives. More than one third estimated positive effect, but approximately every tenth young adults estimated negative effect. Only six per cent of those considering resignation from the Church reported positive experiences. Some young adults considering resignation from the Church had been left with a concrete image of God from childhood and confirmation classes although their thinking had otherwise developed abstractly. Thus it was felt that it was simply stupid of the Church that they had been offered childish faith, they had been told fairytales and that the Church in confirmation classes had acted as if in Sunday school.

The study clearly demonstrates the importance of the home as a source of Christian upbringing. Its influence on the thinking of a young adult is powerful. Religious upbringing in the home, however, has disappeared almost completely from more and more homes, or at least diminished to be very slight. This decrease is especially marked in the metropolitan area. The effects of religious upbringing at home are most influential when both parents are active in it. However, spiritual identity seems to derive very independently without the active influence of religious upbringing. The lack of religious upbringing does not make children non-religious in a broader sense. Only the institutionally and traditionally bound forms of religion suffer. Therefore, the breaking of the chain of memory in the terms of Hervieu-Léger, the decline of religion because of lack of religious upbringing only concerns traditional forms of religion. Urban young adults without religious upbringing at home are still likely to identify themselves as spiritual and therefore to have some kind of relationship with the transcendental.

EPILOGUE

What do Church employees think of young adults?

There is a story in the New Testament with the promise: when two or three of you are gathered in my name… It is from this that we have the variant, which is true to a very large extent "*When two or three Church employees come together, what they talk about is young adults*". Today it is difficult to conceive of a training session or seminar for Church employees which does not in one way or another address the matter of young adults. In order to be successful in Church elections it is advisable to mention as one source of concern the way in which young adults have drifted away from the Church. Not only the Evangelical Lutheran Parishes of Helsinki, but also other large unions of parishes have set up their own project with young adults. The central administrative organ of the Evangelical Lutheran Church of Finland, the Church Council, has initiated a three-year project *The Young Adult as a Member of the Church* intended to coordinate and develop the work with young adults at national level.

The young adults 'question' had thus undeniably made its mark in the Church. The discussion on the increase in the number of those resigning from the Church, and on young adults, however, has not remained solely within the Church. The issue has aroused interest more widely, as it has been the subject of tens of newspaper articles, including the nation's largest quality daily. Experts on Church life and religiosity have been interviewed on television. For example, the publication of the Finnish book *Urbaani usko (Urban Faith)* made the news threshold to the main national TV news. All this attention goes to show how important the position of the Church continues to be in Finnish society.

The position of young adults in the Church

In this book the main attention has been on what young adults think of the Church and their views on religion and spirituality. Here, however, we consider what the clergy working in Helsinki think of young adults and of the challenges they pose for the Church. Why in the opinion of the clergy do young adults leave the Church, and how could the Church strengthen its bonds with the young age groups? Exactly who are these young adults who have come in for so much attention? For this chapter fifteen members of the clergy were interviewed, six of them senior vicars.

For many of the clergy interviewed in the project, the age group included (20–39) felt too wide. An individual almost forty years old is middle aged rather than a young adult. Indeed, the interviewees wondered what the concept of young adult was intended to convey. Opening up the significance of the concept was deemed important from the perspective of the operative conclusions to be drawn in the Church: in what kind of young adults are future efforts by the Church to be invested? The members of the clergy interviewed described the life of a young adult as still in many ways unsettled, a life which according to them still included the freedom of youth and less responsibility than is required in actual adulthood. In addition to freedom, the young adult's life was thought to be characterised by constant change and making far-reaching choices and solutions. This is the time in life when they find a place to work or study, a spouse and consider starting a family. Generally young adults were described as having no families and many were of the opinion that young adulthood ends at the latest when it becomes necessary to shoulder the responsibility for children. It was specifically the young adults with no families who were singled out as a difficult group for the Church to reach. According to the clergy interviewed young adulthood is above all a way of life which is not defined by age as by a certain urban lifestyle: *"A thirty-year-old living in a rural area is not a young adult in the same sense as a citydweller."*

According to the interviewees the main reason for the increase in the numbers of people leaving the Church was a reformed legislation which came into force in 2003. Under this legislation

129

the actual operation of resigning from the Church became considerably easier. Formerly resignation from the Church had to be tendered in person in one's own Church offices, whereas after 2004 notice in writing or even an e-mail sent to the local administrative court suffices. Those people who had been thinking a long time about their Church membership now with the new legislation took a negative decision. However, the interviewees were unanimous that the Church should look behind this "technical" explanation if a change for the better was to be achieved in the resignation statistics.

Many of the interviewees considered it entirely understandable that it should be specifically young adults who are well represented among those leaving the Church. This is the time in life when people cut loose from the childhood family, become independent and construct their own world views. Therefore young adults feel a need to distance themselves from the traditions, values and also the religion their parents stand for. Many interviewees thought that young adults consider the Church's thinking restrictive and in some way dogmatic in matters of faith. This attitude is unpopular since *"a person should nowadays be allowed to form his/her world view for him/herself. There is belief in God, but it's My God."*

In addition to the "protest" against the Church there is the hedonistic way of life acclaimed by young people to alienate them from the Church. According to the interviewees people nowadays spend a great deal of time and money on entertaining themselves. Sports events, concerts and many kinds of hobbies are the situations in which people seek communality and strong sensations. An individual who enjoys entertainment and money takes a short-term view of life and from the perspective of his/her own use. Such an individual easily asks what use it is to be a member of the Church and what s/he really gets in return for the Church taxes s/he pays. According to the clergy this selfish way of thinking, however, runs in principle contrary to Christianity and the Church, as the fundamental issue in paying Church taxes is one of giving, not receiving.

The clergy were ready to concede that the Church, too, is at fault. The Church should be better able to justify to young adults the significance of being a member, as mere tradition is no longer sufficient reason for paying Church taxes. The clergy asked self-critically: how many people would pay membership fees to an organisation with which they have in practice no contact, which does not appear to give anything and whose activities are unknown? A certain way of thinking of the lifespan exerts a very powerful influence in the Church. According to this, life progresses in a logical order from childhood to youth towards adulthood and parenthood. If an individual's life does not progress according to this model the weaknesses in the activities the Church has to offer will be exposed. The activities appreciated by young adults, church rites, presuppose the existence of a spouse and children. In the opinion of many of the clergy the profile of the Church is currently too much that of the church for traditional family values. The Church has not succeeded in catering for the great diversity of urban people's lives. Of the young adults of 20–39 in Helsinki over half (59%) are childless.

The interviewees had grave doubts as to whether the Church employees were ultimately capable of finding such means that would have a positive effect on the Church's membership numbers. With one exception the clergy interviewed thought that the trend of resigning from the Church would continue steadily for at least the next ten years. Not even the interviewee who predicted a growth in Church membership was able to say what would bring this development about. It was the general estimate of the clergy that in 2015 some 60 per cent of Helsinki people would still be members of the Church. Some estimates were much more pessimistic. The worst case scenario was that in ten years' time only a marginal group of Helsinki people would belong to the Church. Many of the interviewees thought that the only thing likely to have a positive effect on Church membership was some major catastrophe. When times are good people appear to get along without the Church, but in the event of a crisis in society or an environmental catastrophe with major implications for Finns, then resignation from the Church would cease and membership would actually increase.

One might pose the critical question, what meaning or sense the clergy could perceive in their own work if it appears to have no significance for the growth of membership. This attitude is understandable against a background in which many of the clergy had themselves experiences of how difficult it is to reach young adults and bring them into the Church's activities. In three Helsinki parishes young adults had actually been approached through a personal letter. A total of 3,800 letters had been sent out, resulting in only seven people being brought into the Church. The interviewees were absolutely unanimous that the regular activities of the parishes do not interest young adults.

The clergy in charge of working with young adults mentioned their own difficult positioning the Church. Their mission was to kindle enthusiasm in such people to join in the activities of the Church who were not initially particularly interested in it. At the same time they had to convince the Church administration how important it is to obtain resources, money and workers in order to bring these lost sheep into the fold. There is no unanimity in the Church regarding how these young adults with questioning minds should be approached. Many Church workers would in the future invest more in active parishioners rather than squandering time and money on currying favour with those whom it is difficult to activate. This view is justified, since it would be very strange if the Church were to have nothing to offer even to those interested in its work. On the other hand such a strategic guideline would mean that the silent majority would be assigned the role of financer. The research permits the prediction that less and less Church tax will be paid while getting nothing in return, thus the Church may not neglect its relations to its passive members.

Several vicars stressed that the problem caused by alienation and resignation from the Church can in no way be solved by further developing activities. If at best the Helsinki parishes were to succeed in doubling the number of active parishioners from the present five percent to ten percent, there would still be 90 per cent beyond the reach of the Church. However, it is to this group that those resigning from the Church mainly belong. Their membership in the Church is determined by factors other than the activities arranged by the parishes. The parish priests moreover noted that a marked increase in the numbers of those active in the parish would soon cause problems relating to resources of space and workers.

What should be done?

The majority of the clergy interviewed were of the opinion that the Church should adopt a client-centred approach. In practice this would mean that activities would basically be planned on the terms of young adults, their needs and their reality. It should be possible to divide young adults into different target groups. Then it would be time to consider what might be offered to each of these groups, as the same methods cannot be employed to reach the heterogeneous young adults.

In practice client-centeredness and target group thinking should ensure that the activities of the Church take place elsewhere than on Church premises. The Church workers should be and go out to where the young adults already are. The research shows that this is something the young adults themselves wanted. The clergy should engage in more networking with the educational institutions, sports clubs, citizens' organisations and workplaces as young adults are very mobile and do not necessarily identify with a certain part of town or their local parish. All in all physical space may be of little significance in the formation of communities. This is exemplified well in the interaction and net communities implemented in the net. The Church has ambitious plans as to how it could "go out" into the net and there involve itself more actively in the discussion on religion and world view. In the next few years it is planned to train Church workers to operate in this virtual parallel reality populated by young adults.

Assimilating a client-centred approach would be justified in the Church for the mere reason alone that the research shows that the values and thought patterns of Church workers differ widely from those of average young adults. The research has shown that Church workers appreciate permanency and responsibility especially highly. They respect tradition, they do not want any change in their lives nor do they pursue enjoyment as an end in itself. From the perspective of the young adults such an attitude is a sign of stagnation, dullness and being old-fashioned. Typically variety and enjoyment are just what young adults want and appreciate. They want many stimuli and action in their lives.

If instead of being client-oriented the Church attempts a worker-centred approach to young adults great success is highly unlikely. The attitudes of Church workers are so remote from the life reality of young adults. It is a great future challenge for the Church to rid itself of an individual, Church worker-centred working culture to assume a mode of operation in which better account is taken of the operating environment. According to one of the vicars interviewed, the Church permits a spectrum of different opinions and views which imbues it with a positive variety of faces. Regrettably this in practice frequently means that workers with different views find it difficult to find common goals for their efforts and to commit to these. Many times workers do what they like regardless of what has been agreed with the superior with regard to the goals and content of the work. The vicar noted in self-criticism that a "busy" way of working was possible due to loose leadership.

The problems of the Church

The clergy interviewed appeared to have a very realistic image of what the Church looks like in the eyes of young adults. To many young adults the Church appears a distant, *passée,* intolerant institution. The main reason for this negative image, according to the interviewees, is that young adults have only little hands-on experience of the Church, so that the image purveyed by the media is accentuated. Many of the clergy interviewed raised the same issues, according to which young adults according to the present research are frequently irritated with the Church. The discussion on the ordaining of women and on sexual minorities as presented in the press and on television does not always convey a flattering picture of the Church. Young adults are particularly sensitive to the occurrence of double morality in the Church: talk of loving one's neighbour, of God's goodness and mercy to all, but at the same time disputing basic rights for women and sexual minorities. The clergy found it regrettable that the small group opposed to women as priests should be granted so much media attention. They also felt that the misdeeds of individual members of the clergy were deliberately featured in the media, likewise the fact that the atmosphere in certain parishes has been shown by some studies to be exceptionally bad. From all this publicity it follows that it is difficult for people to feel that the Church is their own and to identify with its employees.

Although critical of the media, the clergy interviewed acknowledged that the saying *"out of sight, out of mind"* is very apt. In the future the Church will need to invest more effort in positive image and communications. As one vicar put it: *"If we want to make a difference here, we need to be seen."* The interviewees felt that many people had a very shaky idea of what the Church accomplishes and what Church taxes are used for. The Church must be able to let its parishioners know what good things their Church membership involves them in. Such a message is particularly important for those who seldom if ever avail themselves of the services the Church provides.

In addition to its public image and communications, the interviewees stated that the Church also had other problems. The gap between the Church and the cultures taken on board by young adults is so great that a mere mention does not suffice to activate young adults alienated from the Church in its activities. A good and concrete example of the gap between cultures in the opinion of the interviewees is the mass. The traditional Finnish ten o'clock mass on a Sunday morning is so high church that it is difficult for a young adult to feel at home there. If the mass is to be made into a more appealing "product" much must be changed, since from the perspective of the young people it is both boring and is held at the wrong time of day. Moreover, most of the music performed during the mass is totally alien to young adults. Those clergy having to do with young people in particular asked if note could be taken in church of the experience of young adults *"How could the music of the hymns be got to a standard that imparts a feeling of joy rather than of pain?"*

In times past the traditional hymn singing may have been the mainstream culture, but at present it only corresponds to the taste of a very marginal group. In the opinion of the clergy interviewed church musicians in the future might be required to possess a wider knowledge of music and the skill to implement different musical styles.

A good example of a bold and successful experiment was the metal mass arranged in 2006, with novel arrangements of traditional hymns in the style of heavy metal. The metal mass, like other innovations in the Church, has been criticised for causing elements alien to the Church to be brought in. The rejoinder to this criticism was that in some Church circles there is a confusion of content with form and ethics with aesthetics. The mass was part of the Helsinki "Pain" festival, at which world famous heavy bands like Venom and Celtic Frost performed. The mass received ample attention from the major media and was a resounding success: hundreds of attendees were left standing outside the church. The mass was repeated early in 2007, and once again the 800-seater church was packed out. The experiment demonstrated how decisive the role of music can be from the perspective of making the service interesting.

In the opinion of the clergy interviewed it is still fairly easy to make changes to the external form of the mass. What is more difficult than changing the external form and more complicated, however, is how to make the Christian message live in this age. It would appear that what is behind the resignation of many young adults from the Church is simply lack of faith. According to the interviewees it is difficult for many reasons to get a grip on the message the Church proclaims. Firstly, many abstract words are used in church whose content may be vague. For many young adults it is not entirely clear what is meant by the reconciliation of sins, mercy and the love of God. If people do not know what is being talked about, no genuine and meaningful contact can be achieved. One vicar remarked laconically that in church people talk very loosely about human worth and love in a way which imparts nothing concrete to the hearer. Many of the interviewees assumed that the language used in church revealed the difficulty of Church workers in encountering modern people and their questions. The use of words has become one means of hiding and taking refuge from difficult discussion subjects.

Some of the interviewees also raised the question about the extent to which vague use of concepts was symptomatic of the clergy's own confusion. It seemed unclear to many of the clergy interviewed what Christian faith actually meant to them let alone why a person ultimately ought to be a member of the Church. It was interesting that the clergy did not primarily justify the importance of Church membership through the sacraments and the message of salvation. Instead, justification was sought through the diaconial work accomplished by the Church, the work with families and young people, i.e. concrete considerations. Could this be taken as a sign of the secularisation of the Church when the workers themselves to not have sufficient faith in the actual content as a sufficient reason for belonging? Perhaps this also indicates that the pastors are reluctant and cautious about connecting detailed religious views as a requirement for membership. In practice there is freedom in the Church to think in many ways on matters of religion and individual religious views are permissible even among the clergy. The Reverend Antti Kylliäinen, whose controversial doctrinal views have brought him publicity, put in a nutshell the tacitly accepted principle in the Church: *"In matters of doctrine each individual is the supreme authority on his/her own thinking."*

The younger clergy in particular noted that there is a great deal of room for improvement in the discussion culture of the Church, and that there should be more discussion on the meaning of Christian faith. Compared to the university, matters are treated lightly and superficially. Recently the most weighty views on matters of religion seem to have come from outside the Church. Religion has been the theme of many popular theatrical performances and others than Church people have written on their religious views.

Perhaps most attention has been paid to the now retired former left-wing professor of social psychology, a former church critic, Antti Eskola (born 1934), who wrote a trilogy on his religious thinking. At present the "worst" radicals and reformers on the Church and Christianity would appear to be in Finland, as elsewhere, slightly older men. Both the American retired Episcopal bishop, John Shelby Spong (born 1931), and the former Scottish archbishop, Richard Holloway (born 1933), have come as far as Finland to stir up a religious debate with their unconventional thoughts.

According to the younger clergy, easy circumstances and concentrating on many kinds of activities has led to a situation in which matters of content have not been contemplated. There is a great deal of activity, but what makes this Christian is frequently unclear, likewise its ultimate objective. According to one vicar there is a need in the Church for profound discussion, otherwise the risk exists that the Church will lose its credibility. Many of the interviewees had the impression that especially among the better educated there exists a suspicion of intellectual dishonesty towards the Church.

In the opinion of the clergy interviewed, the Church should be openly asking together with the young adults what the purpose of life is, likewise the values on which it is possible to build a good life. Many of the clergy voiced harsh societal criticism: "*A great deal of humanity has been sacrificed at the altar of the competitive society, that is results have been achieved at the expense of humanity... people are exploited, then when there is no more to exploit they are cast off. This says nothing good about the spiritual state of our society.*" In a society which at present appears to be built on money and success, the Church offers a different perspective. Each individual has an undeniable value regardless of his/her success in life, whether such success be economic, in human relations or in the ability to live according to Christian ideals. To those who in their lives have encountered incompleteness, failure and disappointment the Church offers support, comfort and hope which in the last instance prevails in the face of death. With Christian faith a person can live even when wounded. The clergy believe that a Christian conviction enables a person to live a responsible life and the ability to make those choices which endure. Thus the Church should serve as an example and be bold in taking a stand on both environmental and social issues and in these be on the side of the weak.

Perceiving what is essential and focussing on it is the major challenge for the Church in the future. Thus resources are diminishing and not everything can be attempted if employees are to be saved from burnout. It is important for the success of the work to be done by the Church that the results of the present research should not be left at the level of theoretical contemplation and talk. The saying quoted at the beginning of this chapter can also be seen as criticism that there has been quite sufficient talk about "problems". Now is the time to set about those indispensable measures which will make it possible for the Church to be a significant part of Finnish culture in the future and of its spiritual life.

Lasse Halme, head of the Parish Union of Helsinki educational and parish services presented in the book *Urbaani usko (Urban Faith)* a list of measures which the Church ought to undertake on the basis of the research findings obtained.[1]

1. Support must be provided for Christian upbringing in the home. The significance of the home is crucial, compared, for example, to school and parish.

2. The content and implementation of confirmation classes must be brought into focus. A surprisingly large number have found the influence of confirmation classes to be negative, and the reasons for this need to be ascertained. Confirmation classes and youth work in the parish should provide a foundation for subsequent connection to the parish. Matters should be handled in such a way as to withstand criticism ten years hence.

3. The educational work of the Church lays the foundation for participation at a later age; participation in youth work especially shows in church attendance at a later age. The content of education should be such that a person feels s/he owns it as an adult, too: a child may not understand everything, but things should be presented consistently to those of different ages. For example, the Bible should be approached and taught at different ages on the basis of the same essential view even if the matters to be processed are different.

4. The connection between the work with young people and with adults must be strengthened. At present there is a gap between these into which the young adults fall. Careful note should be taken in the parishes of the fact that half of the parishioners may well be in the age group 20–39. This should be reflected in activities and participation.

5. The criticism levelled by young adults at the services and music life should be taken seriously. This will lead to the implementation of different services and a wide variety of music and culture. This musical language must be seriously considered in the training of church

---

1   Halme 2006, 342–356.

musicians and the parishes must have positions and cantors for this purpose.

6. Church rites will continue to be among the cornerstones and their implementation requires constant attention. The Church rites of the parishes are to be seen as strategic strengths around which many other types of links can be forged to parishioners. Special attention must be paid to the ways in which encounter and interaction take place.

7. Those moving into the parish should be catered for in a modern and interesting way. A change in the stage of life provides an opportunity for personal contact. Blessing the home is an opportunity to join in the lives of the new arrivals and the parishes should develop activities and actively offer opportunities to bless the home. Kallio is the gateway to Helsinki, and this should be noted by the Helsinki parishes as a whole. In the areas of young adults the diaconal work can be directed towards young adults' life management, and matters pertaining to studies and working life. The parish should build communality in the areas where there is migration.

8. Those joining the Church should be personally acknowledged. They should be offered individual and group meetings and opportunities to intensify their Church membership and the meaning of Christianity in their own lives.

9. The new spirituality should be taken seriously and alternative forms of Church activity developed, services and devotions. The painting courses and retreats in the parish of Kallio open up promising opportunities in this direction. Young adults are not a monolithic group, and this diversity must be taken into consideration. The needs of young adults should be taken into account in the decisions taken regarding premises.

10. Seen from the perspective of the Church the thinking of the young adults of Kallio is far from conservative Christianity, and rather liberal Christianity, thus strict stands taken by the Church will have a negative effect on their image of the Church. The Church must set a course between the conservative and liberal lines and the choice is to be taken in the direction of young adults.

11. The views and questions of young adults must be heeded and the activities of the parishes adapted accordingly. The areas of life which are important to young adults are those pertaining to identity, the pair relationship and family, likewise the community and exerting influence. The Church must immediately provide something in return for the Church taxes paid by young adults. In addition to immediate benefit it is important to stress that members of the Church support all kinds of Church activity for the benefit of people of different ages. For hundreds of years the Church has been building Finnish society, and its significance to Finnish culture is great. Members are in-

volved in the conservation of this cultural tradition and are carrying it forward.

12. Pair relationship activities targeted at young adults, for example *"Chemistry between us"* courses for young couples open up a new opportunity for work with young adults and this must be purposefully developed. Family counselling provides an opportunity to process problems in the pair relationship.

13. It is in the interests of the Church as a whole that the proportion of young adults in Church decision-making should increase. The challenge of young adults should be taken into account in the training and recruitment of workers.

14. There is a need for serious theological work and dialogue to connect the Christian tradition and the lives of young adults. The Church should not go along with consumer ideology; in keeping with the principles of the Reformation the parish should constantly be renewing itself. The basic tenets of Christianity can be found and expressed in a fresh and meaningful way.

15. Good quantity and quality of communications should ensure that young adults know about the activities of the parish and that the public image of the Church is in good order.

BIBLIOGRAPHY

Aldén Ann
2005 The Religiosity/Spirituality. Lecture transpariens. [http://www.ceuc.org/liselund/Overheadblad%203.doc]

Alden, Ann
2006 Religion in Dialogue With Late Modern Society: A Constructive Contribution to a Christian Spirituality Informed by Buddhist-Christian Encounters. Peter Lang Publishing Inc.

Alestalo, Matti
1985 Yhteiskuntaluokat ja sosiaaliset kerrostumat toisen maailmansodan jälkeen – Tapani Valkonen & Matti Alestalo & Riitta Jallinoja & Tom Sandlund Suomalaiset. Yhteiskunnan rakenne teollistumisen aikana. Neljäs painos. Juva: WSOY, s. 101–200.

Anttiroiko, Ari-Veikko & Aro, Jari & Karvonen, Erkki
2000 Tietoyhteiskunnan oppihistorialliset lähtökohdat – Matti Vuorensyrjä & Reijo Savolainen (eds.) Tieto ja tietoyhteiskunta. Helsinki: Gaudeamus, s. 21–41.

Arnett, Jeffrey Jensen
2000 Emerging Adulthood. A Theory of Development From the Late Teens through the Twenties. American Psychologist. Vol 55, No. 5, 469–480.

Arnett, Jeffrey Jensen
2004 Adolescence and Emerging Adulthood. A Cultural Approach. Second Edition. New Jersey: Pearson.

Bahr, Howard
1970 Aging and religious disaffiliation. – Social Forces 49, 60–71.

Bauman, Zygmunt
1996 Postmodernin lumo. Toimittaneet Pirkkoliisa Ahponen & Timo Cantell. Tampere: Vastapaino.

Bauman, Zygmunt
2002 Notkea moderni. Tampere: Vastapaino.

Beck, Ulrich
1995 Politiikan uudelleen keksiminen. Kohti refleksiivisen modernisaation
[1994] teoriaa – Ulrich Beck & Anthony Giddens & Scott Lash Nykyajan jäljillä. Refleksiivinen modernisaatio. Tampere: Vastapaino, s. 11–82.

Bell, Daniel
1974 The Coming of Post-Industrial Society. A Venture in Social Forecasting. London: Heinemann.

Berger, Peter L. & Berger, Brigitte & Kellner Hansfried
1977   The Homeless Mind. Modernization and Consciousness. Harmonds-
[1973]   worth: Penguin Books.

Beyer, Peter
1994   Religion and Globalization. London: Sage.

Brooks, David
2001   Bobos en el paraíso. Ni hippies ni yuppies: un retrato de la nueva cla-
[2000]   se triunfadora. Traducción de Bettina Blanch Tyroller. Barcelona:
         Grijalbo Mondadori.

Camus, Albert
1971   Kapinoiva ihminen. Esseitä ja katkelmia. Helsinki: Otava.

Cantell, Timo
2006   Nuorten aikuisten Kallio – Teija Mikkola & Kati Niemelä & Juha
         Petterson (eds.) Urbaani usko. Nuoret aikuiset, usko ja kirkko. Kir-
         kon tutkimuskeskuksen julkaisuja 96. Tampere: Kirkon tutkimuskes-
         kus, s. 12–22.

Casanova, José
1994   Public Religion in the Modern World. Chicago: The University of
         Chicago Press.

Chaves, Mark
1991   Family Structure and Protestant Church Attendance: The Sociological
         Basis of Cohort and Age Effects. – Journal for the Scientific Study of
         Religion 30, 501–514.

Coupland, Douglas
1992   Tuntematon sukupolvi. Tarinoita kiihtyvästä kulttuurista. Juva:
         WSOY.

Davie, Grace
1994   Religion in Britain since 1945: Believing Without Belonging.
         Oxford: Blackwell.

Davie, Grace
2000   Religion in Modern Europe. A Memory Mutates. Oxford: Oxford
         University Press.
2006   Is Europe an Exceptional Case? – After Secularization. The Hedge-
         hog Review: Critical Reflections on Contemporary Culture,
         Spring/Summer 2006, 23–34.

Durkheim, Émile
1980   Uskontoelämän alkeismuodot. Australialainen toteemijärjestelmä.
[1912]   Helsinki: Tammi.

Durkheim, Émile
1985   Itsemurha. Sosiologinen tutkimus. Helsinki: Tammi.
[1897]

1990   Sosiaalisesta työnjaosta. Helsinki: Gaudeamus.
[1893]

Ferrara, Alessandro
1998   Reflective Authenticity. Rethinking the Project of Modernity. London & New York: Routledge.

Fischter, Josep
1954   Social Relations in the Urban Parish. Chicago & London: The University of Chicago Press.

Florida, Richard
2005   Luovan luokan esiinmarssi. Miten se muuttaa työssäkäyntiä, vapaa-aikaa, yhteiskuntaa ja arkielämää. Helsinki: Talentum.

Fromm, Erich
1965   Ihmisen osa. Helsinki: Kirjayhtymä.
[1947]
1967   Hyvän ja pahan välillä. Helsinki: Kirjayhtymä
[1964]
1971   Terve yhteiskunta. Helsinki: Kirjayhtymä.
1986   Psykoanalyysi ja uskonto. Helsinki: Kirjayhtymä.
[1990]

Furnham, Adrian
1996   The Protestant Work Ethic. The Psychology of Work-Related Beliefs
[1990]   and Behaviours. London: Whurr Publishers.

Giddens, Anthony
1991   Modernity and Self-Identity. Self and Society in the Late Modern Age. Cambridge: Polity Press.
1994   Beyond Left and Right. The Future of Radical Politics. Cambridge: Polity Press.
1995   Elämää jälkitraditionaalisessa yhteiskunnassa – Ulrich Beck & Anthony Giddens & Scott Lash Nykyajan jäljillä. Refleksiivinen modernisaatio. Tampere: Vastapaino, s. 82–152.
1999   Runaway World. How Globalisation is Reshaping our Lives. London: Profile Books.
2000   The Third Way. The Renewal of Social Democracy. Cambridge:
[1998]   Polity Press.
          Gollnick, James
2005   Religion and Spirituality in the Life Cycle. New York/Washington/Baltimore/Bern/Frankfurt am Main/Berlin/Brussels/Vienna/Oxford: Peter Lang.

Grünstein, Raoul
2005   Luovuuden mallimaa? In Florida, Richard. Luovan luokan esiinmarssi. Miten se muuttaa työssäkäyntiä, vapaa-aikaa, yhteiskuntaa ja arkielämää. Helsinki: Talentum. 11–17.

Grönlund, Henrietta
2006   Nuoret aikuiset kirkon vapaaehtoistoiminnassa. Arvostukset, asenteet ja aktivointi – Teija Mikkola, Kati Niemelä & Juha Petterson (eds.) Urbaani usko. Nuoret aikuiset, usko ja kirkko. Kirkon tutkimuskeskuksen julkaisuja 96. Tampere: Kirkon tutkimuskeskus, 118–133.

Gustafsson, Göran & Pettersson, Thorleif (eds.)
2000   Folkkyrkor och religiös pluralism – den nordiska reliösa modellen. Stockholm: Verbum.

Haikonen, Jyrki & Kiljunen, Pentti
2003   Mitä mieltä, suomalainen? EVAn asennetutkimuksien kertomaa vuosilta 1984–2003. Helsinki: Taloustieto Oy.

Halme, Lasse
2006   Nuorten aikuisten haaste kirkolle – Johtopäätöksiä nuorten aikuisten projektista – Teija Mikkola, Kati Niemelä & Juha Petterson (eds.) Urbaani usko. Nuoret aikuiset, usko ja kirkko. Kirkon tutkimuskeksuksen julkaisuja 96. Tampere: Kirkon tutkimuskeskus, 342–356.

Halme, Lasse & Mikkola, Teija & Niemelä, Kati & Petterson, Juha
2006   Johdanto – Teija Mikkola, Kati Niemelä & Juha Petterson (eds.) Urbaani usko. Nuoret aikuiset, usko ja kirkko. Kirkon tutkimuskeksuksen julkaisuja 96. Tampere: Kirkon tutkimuskeskus,

Harvola, Heikki
2006   Nuoret aikuiset seurakunnan maalauskursseilla – Teija Mikkola, Kati Niemelä & Juha Petterson (eds.) Urbaani usko. Nuoret aikuiset, usko ja kirkko. Kirkon tutkimuskeskuksen julkaisuja 96. Tampere: Kirkon tutkimuskeskus, 134–147.

Heelas, Paul
2002   The spiritual revolution: from 'religion' to 'spirituality' – Religions in the modern world: Traditions and transformations. Linda Woodhead & Paul Fletcher & Hiroko Kawanami & David Smith (eds.). London/New York: Routledge. 357–377.

Heelas, Paul & Linda Woodhead (in association with Benjamin Steel & Bronislaw Szerzynski & Karin Tusting)
2005   The Spiritual Revolution: Why Religion Is Giving Way to Spirituality. Oxford: Blackwell.

Helkama, Klaus & Myllyniemi, Rauni & Liebkind, Karmela
1998   Johdatus sosiaalipsykologiaan. Helsinki: Edita.

Hervieu-Léger, Danièle
2000   Religion as a Chain of Memory. Trans. Simon Lee. Cambridge: Polity Press.

Hoikkala, Tommi
1989   Nuorisokulttuurista kulttuuriseen nuoruuteen. Helsinki: Gaudeamus.

1993   Katoaako kasvatus, himmeneekö aikuisuus. Aikuistumisen puhe- ja kulttuurisia malleja. Helsinki: Gaudeamus.

1994   Joksikin tuleminen ja nuorten itsenäistymisen ongelma – Keijo Voudinmäki (ed.) Tulla joksikin. Helsinki: WSOY, 183–190.

Hoikkala, Tommi & Laine, Sofia & Laine, Jyrki
2005   Johdanto. Nuorison kapina ja suomalaiset sukupolvet – Tommi Hoikkala & Sofia Laine & Jyrki Laine (eds.) Mitä on tehtävä? Nuorison kapinan teoriaa ja käytäntöä. Helsinki: Nuorisotutkimusverkosto/Nuorisotutkimusseura, julkaisuja 52, 9–22.

Hunt, Stephen
2005   Religion and Everyday Life. London/New York: Routledge.

HS 29.11.2004.
2004   Helsingin Sanomat 29.11.2004. Suomalaisten ja ranskalaisten arvot lähellä toisiaan, Kotimaa, Hannele Tarkka-Tierala.

HS 20.03.2005
2005   D8 Kalliosta ei vieläkään päästä, Tomi Ervamaa.

Hyvönen, Jenni
2006   Urbaanin kristityn nuoren aikuisen spiritualiteetti – Teija Mikkola, Kati Niemelä & Juha Petterson (eds.) Urbaani usko. Nuoret aikuiset, usko ja kirkko. Kirkon tutkimuskeskuksen julkaisuja 96. Tampere: Kirkon tutkimuskeskus, 84–103.

Inglehart, Ronald
1997   Modernization and Postmodernization. Cultural, economic, and political change in 43 societies. New Jersey: Princeton University Press.

Inglehart, Ronald & Baker, Wayne E
2000   Modernization, Cultural Change, and the Persistence of Traditional Values. – American Sociological Review 65 (1)/2000. 19–51.

Inglehart, Ronald & Norris, Pippa
2003   Rising Tide. Gender Equality and Cultural Change around the World. Cambridge: Cambridge University Press.

Jallinoja, Riitta
1991   Moderni elämä. Ajankuva ja käytäntö. Suomalaisen Kirjallisuuden Seuran toimituksia 550. Helsinki: SKS.

Ketola, Kimmo
2006   Kaupunkien uusi henkisyys –Teija Mikkola & Kati Niemelä & Juha Petterson (eds.) Urbaani usko. Nuoret aikuiset, usko ja kirkko. Kirkon tutkimuskeskuksen julkaisuja 96. Tampere: Kirkon tutkimuskeskus, s. 305–330.

Kipnis, Laura
2005   Avioliiton ansa. Helsinki: Like.

Kirkko muutosten keskellä
2004   Suomen evankelis-luterilainen kirkko vuosina 2000–2003. Kirkon tutkimuskeskuksen julkaisuja 89. Tampere: Kirkon tutkimuskeskus.

Kirkon tilastollinen vuosikirja
2005   Helsinki: Kirkkohallitus

Kortteinen, Matti
1982   Lähiö. Tutkimus elämäntapojen muutoksesta. Helsinki: Otava.

Kosunen, Emilia
2006   Nuorten miesten mysteeri. Kirkosta eronneiden nuorten miesten spiri-tualiteetti – Teija Mikkola, Kati Niemelä & Juha Petterson (eds.) Urbaani usko. Nuoret aikuiset, usko ja kirkko. Kirkon tutkimuskes-kuksen julkaisuja 96. Tampere: Kirkon tutkimuskeskus, 263–277.

Kumpulainen, Ilona & Gothoni, Raili
2006   Nuoret nopeatempoiset monitoimijat – Teija Mikkola, Kati Niemelä & Juha Petterson (eds.) Urbaani usko. Nuoret aikuiset, usko ja kirk-ko. Kirkon tutkimuskeskuksen julkaisuja 96. Tampere: Kirkon tutkimuskeskus, 250–262.

Kääriäinen, Kimmo & Niemelä, Kati & Ketola, Kimmo
2003   Moderni kirkkokansa. Suomalaisten uskonnollisuus uudella vuositu-hannella. Kirkon tutkimuskeskuksen julkaisuja 82. Kirkon tutkimus-keskuksen julkaisuja 96. Tampere: Kirkon tutkimuskeskus.

Kääriäinen, Kimmo & Niemelä Kati & Ketola Kimmo
2005   Religion in Finland: Decline, Change, and Transformation of Finnish Religiosity. Publications of the Church Research Institute 54. Tampe-re: The Church Research Institute.

Luckmann, Thomas
1967   The Invisible Religion: the Problem of Religion in the Modern Society. New York: Macmillan.

Lyon, David
1995   Postmodernity. Buckingham: Open University Press.
[1994]

Lyotard, Jean-Francois
1985   Tieto postmodernissa yhteiskunnassa. Tampere: Vastapaino.
[1979]

Majamäki, Hannu
2006   Nuoret aikuiset ja kirkko – mahdollinen yhtälö? – Teija Mikkola, Kati Niemelä & Juha Petterson (eds.) Urbaani usko. Nuoret aikuiset, usko ja kirkko. Kirkon tutkimuskeskuksen julkaisuja 96. Tampere: Kirkon tutkimuskeskus, 332–341.

Mikkola, Teija
2003   Muuttuvat arvot ja uusi keskiluokka. Tutkimus arvojen mittaamisesta ja monitasoisuudesta. Helsingin yliopiston sosiologian laitoksen tutkimuksia No. 241. Electronic publication: [http://ethesis.helsinki.fi/julkaisut/val/sosio/vk/mikkola/]

Mikkola, Teija
2005   Uudenaikainen uskonnollisuus – Teologinen aikakauskirja 4/2005. 359–376.

Mikkola, Teija
2006   Urbaanin nuoren aikuisen arvot –Teija Mikkola & Kati Niemelä & Juha Petterson (eds.) Urbaani usko. Nuoret aikuiset, usko ja kirkko. Kirkon tutkimuskeskuksen julkaisuja 96. Tampere: Kirkon tutkimuskeskus, s. 23–42.

Mitchell, Arnold
1983   The Nine American Lifestyles. Who We Are & Where We Are Going. New York: Macmillan.

Moberg, David O.
2002   Religion and Spirituality – Social Compass vol 49 mun. 1. 133–138.

Mäenpää, Pasi
2003   Mitä nuoret edellä... – Sonja Kangas & Tapio Kuure (eds.) Teknologisoituva nuoruus. Yliopistopaino, Helsinki.

Mäenpää, Pasi
2005   Narkissos kaupungissa. Tutkimus kuluttaja-kaupunkilaisesta ja julkisesta tilasta. Helsinki: Tammi.

Mäenpää, Pasi
2006   Urbaani elämäntapa ja sen uusi uskonnollisuus. – Teija Mikkola & Kati Niemelä & Juha Petterson (eds.) Urbaani usko. Nuoret aikuiset, usko ja kirkko. Kirkon tutkimuskeskuksen julkaisuja 96. Tampere: Kirkon tutkimuskeskus, s. 317–330.

Niemelä, Kati
2002   Hyvä rippikoulu. Rippikoulun laatu ja vaikuttavuus. Kirkon tutkimuskeskus, Sarja A Nro 79. Tampere: Kirkon tutkimuskeskus.

Niemelä, Kati
2004   Uskonko niin kuin opetan? Seurakuntatyöntekijä uskon ja elämän ristipaineessa. Kirkon tutkimuskeskuksen julkaisuja 85. Tampere: Kirkon tutkimuskeskus.

Niemelä, Kati
2006   Vieraantunut vai pettynyt? Kirkosta eroamisen syyt Suomen evankelis-luterilaisessa kirkossa. Kirkon tutkimuskeskuksen julkaisuja 95. Tampere: Kirkon tutkimuskeskus.

Niemelä, Kati
2006b   Nuorten aikuisten suhde kirkkoon. – Teija Mikkola & Kati Niemelä & Juha Petterson (eds.) Urbaani usko. Nuoret aikuiset, usko ja kirkko. Kirkon tutkimuskeskuksen julkaisuja 96. Tampere: Kirkon tutkimuskeskus, s. 43–65.

Niemelä, Kati
2006c   The quality and effectiveness of confirmation classes in Finland. – Journal of Beliefs & Values. Vol. 27, No. 2, August 2006, 177–190.

Niemelä, Kati
2006d   Does Religous Upbringing Matter? The effect of religious upbringing on the religious and spiritual identity of urban young adults in Finland. – Kirsi Tirri (ed.) Religion, spirituality & identity. Peter Lang Publ Inc, 153–169.

Niemelä, Kati
[in press] Alienated or disappointed? Reasons for leaving the Church in Finland. Will be published in Nordic Journal of Religion and Society 2/2007.

Nietzsche, Friedrich
1995   Näin puhui Zarathustra. Kirja kaikille eikä kenellekään. Helsinki:
[1883–   Otava.
1891]

Nietzsche, Friedrich
1997   Iloinen tiede. Helsinki: Otava.
[1882]

Nousiainen, Jaakko
1992   Suomen poliittinen järjestelmä. Porvoo, Helsinki, Juva: WSOY.

Ortega y Gasset, José
1963   Massojen kapina. Toinen painos. Helsinki: Otava
[n.d.]

Paajanen, Pirjo
2002   Saako haikara tulla käymään? Suomalaisten lastenhankinnan ihanteet ja todellisuus. Väestöntutkimuslaitos, Katsauksia E 14/2002. Helsinki: Väestöliitto.

Perttula, Juha
2001   Olenko onnellinen? Psykologista tunnustelua suomalaisen aikuisen onnellisuudesta. Jyväskylä: PS-kustannus.

Pietarinen, Juhani
1994   Itsemäärääminen ja itsemääräämisoikeus – Juhani Pietarinen & Veikko Launis & Juha Räikkä & Eerik Lagerspetz & Marjo Rauhala & Markku Oksanen Oikeus itsemääräämiseen. Helsinki: Painatuskeskus. 15–47.

Pohjanheimo, Esa
2005   Pysyvää ja eriytyvää. Arvomuutoksia Suomessa 1970-luvulta nyky-päivään. – Anna-Maija Pirttilä-Backman & Marja Ahokas & Liisa Myyry & Susanna Lähteenoja (eds.) Arvot, moraali ja yhteiskunta. Sosiaalipsykologisia näkökulmia yhteiskunnan muutokseen. Helsinki: Gaudeamus. 237–257.

Puohiniemi, Martti
1993   Suomalaisten arvot ja tulevaisuus. Analyysi väestön ja vaikuttajien näkemyksistä. Valtioneuvoston selonteko eduskunnalle pitkän aika-välin tulevaisuudesta. Valtioneuvoston kanslian julkaisusarja 1993/5, Tilastokeskus tutkimuksia 202. Helsinki.

Ray, Paul H. & Anderson, Ruth
2000   The Cultural Creatives. How 50 Million People Are Changing the World. New York: Harmony Books

Reich, Charles A.
1972   Uuteen maailmaan. Helsinki: Kirjayhtymä.
[1970]

Rantala, Onni
1960   Konservatismi ja sen kannattajat. Helsinki: Tammi.

Riesman, David (in collaboration with Reuel Denney & Nathan Glazer)
1953   The Lonely Crowd. A Study of the Changing American Character.
[1950]   Fifth Printing. New Haven: Yale University Press.

RISC Monitor perusraportti 2002
2002   Perus- ja trendiraportti. Helsinki: MDC Risc International

Roof, Wade Clark
2003   Religion and Spirituality: Toward an Integrated Analysis. – Michele Dillon (ed.) Handbook of the Sociology of Religion. Cambridge: Cambridge University Press. 137–148.

Saastamoinen, Kari
1998   Eurooppalainen liberalismi. Etiikka, talous, politiikka. Jyväskylä: Atena.

Saliba, John A.
1995   Religious Dimensions of Ufo Phenomena – James r. Lewis (ed.) The Gods Have Landed. New Religions from Other Worlds. Albany: State University of New York Press, pp. 15–64.

Schulze, Gerhard
1992   Die Erlebnisgesellschaft: Kultursoziologie der Gegenwart. Frankfurt am Main: Campus.

Schwartz, Shalom
1992   Universals in the Content and Structure of Values. Theoretical Advances and Empirical Tests in 20 Countries – Mark Zanna (ed.) Advances in Experimental Social Psychology, 25. San Diego: Acade-mic Press, pp. 1–65.

Schwartz, Shalom
1992   Universals in the Content and Structure of Values. Theoretical Advances and Empirical Tests in 20 Countries" –Mark Zanna (ed.) Advances in Experimental Social Psychology, 25 . San Diego: Academic Press, pp. 1–65.

Schwartz, Shalom & Bilsky, Wolfgang
1987   Toward a Universal Psychological Structure of Human Values – Journal of Personality and Social Psychology 53 (3):550–562.
1990   Toward a Theory of the Universal Content and Structure of Values. Extensions and Cross-Cultural Replications – Journal of Personality and Social Psychology 58 (5):878–891.

Sennet, Richard
2002   Työn uusi järjestys. Miten uusi kapitalismi kuluttaa ihmisen luonnetta. Tampere: Vastapaino.

Sheehy, Gail
1977   Vaaralliset vuodet. Aikuisiän kriisit. Helsinki: Tammi.
[1974]

Sihvo, Jouko
1979   Uskonnollisuus ja kirkollisuus Suomessa. Tampere: Kirkon tutkimuslaitos sarja A N:o 34.

Sihvo, Jouko
1992   Seurakunta elämän käännekohdissa. Pieksämäki: Sisälähetysseuran kirjapaino Raamattutalo.

Siltala, Johanna
2005   Parisuhteen kaipaus ja täyttymys – Kallion nuorten aikuisten parisuhdekäsitykset. Käytännöllisen teologian pro gradu -tutkielma. HYTTK.

Siltala, Johanna
2006   Kallion nuorten aikuisten parisuhdekäsitykset ja toiveet kirkon parisuhdetyölle – Teija Mikkola, Kati Niemelä & Juha Petterson (eds.) Urbaani usko. Nuoret aikuiset, usko ja kirkko. Kirkon tutkimuskeskuksen julkaisuja 96. Tampere: Kirkon tutkimuskeskus. 148–162.

Simmel, Georg
2005   Suurkaupunki ja moderni elämä. Kirjoituksia vuosilta 1895–1917. Helsinki: Gaudeamus.

Smart, Ninian
2005   Uskontojen maailma. Keuruu: Otava.

Stakes Tilastotiedote 21
2005   Synnyttäjät, synnytykset ja vastasyntyneet 2004. SVT 12.10.2005. Terveys 2005.

Sundback, Susan
2000   Medlemskapet i de lutherska kyrkorna i Norden. – Gustafsson, Göran & Pettersson, Thorleif (eds.) Folkkyrkor och religiös pluralism – den nordiska reliösa modellen. Stockholm: Verbum.

Svendsen, Lars. Fr. H.
2005   Ikävystymisen filosofiaa. Helsinki: Tammi.

Taira, Teemu & Väliaho Pasi.
2006   "Virtuaalinen" – Uuden työn sanakirja. Helsinki: Tutkijaliitto.

Taylor, Charles
1995   Autenttisuuden etiikka. Helsinki: Gaudeamus.
[1991]

Tirri, Kirsi
2006   Nuorten aikuisten spiritualiteetti Kalliossa. – Teija Mikkola & Kati Niemelä & Juha Petterson (eds.) Urbaani usko. Nuoret aikuiset, usko ja kirkko. Kirkon tutkimuskeskuksen julkaisuja 96. Tampere: Kirkon tutkimuskeskus, s. 292–304

Torvi, Kai & Kiljunen, Pentti
2005   Onnellisuuden vaikea yhtälö. EVAn kansallinen arvo- ja asennetutkimus 2005. Helsinki: Taloustieto Oy.

Uskon asia. Nuorisobarometri
2006   Ed. Terhi-Anna Wilska. Nuorisoasiain neuvottelukunta, julkaisuja 34; Nuorisotutkimusverkosto/Nuorisotutkimusseura julkaisuja 67. Helsinki: Opetusministeriö, Nuorisotutkimusverkosto, Nuorisoasiain neuvottelukunta. Julkaistu sähköisessä muodossa [http://www.minedu.fi/OPM/Nuoriso/nuorisoasiain_neuvottelukunta/julkaisut/barometrit/liitteet/Nuorisobarometri_2006.pdf]

Vattimo, Gianni
1999   Uskon että uskon. Suomentanut Juhani Vähämäki. Jyväskylä: Nemo.

Venkula, Jaana & Rautevaara, Ahti
1992   Arvot ja nuorten arvopohdinta. Piirteitä maamme vv. 1960–1990 nuorten arvoja koskevista tutkimuksista. Helsinki: Yliopistopaino.

Väestö 2005:5
2005   Väestörakenne ja väestömuutokset kunnittain 2004. SVT. Helsinki: Tilastokeskus.

Wathen, Elisa
2006   Edes kerran vuodessa kirkkoon. – Teija Mikkola & Kati Niemelä & Juha Petterson (eds.) Urbaani usko. Nuoret aikuiset, usko ja kirkko. Kirkon tutkimuskeskuksen julkaisuja 96. Tampere: Kirkon tutkimuskeskus, 178–189.

Weber, Max
1989   Maailmanuskonnot ja moderni länsimainen rationaalisuus. Kirjoituk-
[pos-   sia uskonnonsosiologiasta. Tampere: Vastapaino.
tuumi,
1920]

Whitmore, John
1995.   Religious Dimensions of the Ufo Abductee Experience –James R.
         Lewis (ed.) The Gods Have Landed. New Religions from Other
         Worlds. Albany: State University of New York Press, 65–84.

Wirth, Louis
1938   Urbanism as a way of life – American Journal of Sociology, 44, 3–24

Wuthnow, Robert
1988   The Restructuring of American Religion: Society and Faith Since
         World War II. Princeton, NJ: Princeton University Press.

Wuthnow, Robert
1998   After Heaven: Spirituality in America since the 1950s. Berkeley: Uni-
         versity of California Press.

Yankelovich, Daniel
1981   New Rules. Searching for Self-Fulfillment in a World Turned Upside
         Down. New York: Random House.
1994   How Changes in the Economy Are Reshaping American Values. –
         Henry J. Aaron & Thomas E. Mann & Timothy Taylor (eds.) Values
         and Public Policy. Washington, D.C: The Brookings Institution.
         16–53.

Yankelovich, Daniel & Zetterberg Hans & Strümpel Burkhard & Shanks Mi-
chael & Immerwahr John & Noelle-Neumann, Elisabeth & Sengoku Tomatsu
& Yuchtman-Yaar Ephraim.
1985   Work and Human Values: An International Report. – Yankelovich et
         al. The World at Work. An International Report on Jobs, Productivity
         and Human Values. New York: Octagon Books. 3–130.

APPENDICES

Appendix 1. Importance of religion among young adults in the metropolitan area. Source: Telephone surveys Religiosity among Young Adults in the Metropolitan Area 2004 and Religiosity among Young Adults in Kallio. %.

Young adults in metropolitan area	Very important	Quite important	Some-what important	Only a little important	Not important	Total	N
Men	10	14	27	25	24	100	493
Women	13	16	30	27	14	100	487
Aged 20-29	10	13	26	30	21	100	515
Aged 30-39	13	18	30	21	18	100	485
Church members	9	17	32	29	14	100	783
Members of other religious organisations	57	15	14	8	4	100	52
Non-Church members	7	7	13	19	54	100	165
Total	11	15	28	26	20	100	1000
Young adults in Kallio	7	13	20	23	37	100	500

Appendix 2. Folk beliefs (young adults in the metropolitan area 2004; N=1,000 of which N=55 for those resident in Kallio; and Church Monitor 2004; N=2,569).

	Beliefs firmly			Considers probable			Does not believe at all		
	Kallio	Hel-sinki area	Fin-land	Kallio	Hel-sinki area	Fin-land	Kallio	Hel-sinki area	Fin-land
Ghosts exist	7	5	2	9	6	9	49	54	63
Another person's life can be influenced by witchcraft	9	5	2	7	6	10	46	51	56
Mediums are able to convey messages from the dead	2	3	2	7	5	9	60	62	54
UFOs exist	11	8	2	16	10	11	32	40	50
A person's future can be predicted by astrology and horoscopes	2	2	1	6	4	8	64	61	51
A person's future can be predicted from playing cards	0	1	1	4	2	4	80	79	66